Abortion beyond the Law

Abortion beyond the Law

Building a Global Feminist Movement for Self-Managed Abortion

Naomi Braine

London • New York

First published by Verso 2023

1 3 5 7 9 10 8 6 4 2

Verso
UK: 6 Meard Street, London W1F 0EG
US: 388 Atlantic Avenue, Brooklyn, NY 11217
versobooks.com

Verso is the imprint of New Left Books

ISBN-13: 978-1-80429-206-8
ISBN-13: 978-1-80429-207-5 (US EBK)
ISBN-13: 978-1-80429-208-2 (UK EBK)

British Library Cataloguing in Publication Data
A catalogue record for this book is available from the British Library

Library of Congress Cataloging-in-Publication Data

Names: Braine, Naomi, author.
Title: Abortion beyond the law : building a global feminist movement for self-managed abortion / Naomi Braine.
Description: London ; New York : Verso, 2023. | Includes bibliographical references and index.
Identifiers: LCCN 2023022292 (print) | LCCN 2023022293 (ebook) | ISBN 9781804292068 (paperback) | ISBN 9781804292075 (ebk)
Subjects: LCSH: Abortion—Political aspects, | Abortion—Law and legislation. | Self-management (Psychology) | Feminism.
Classification: LCC HQ767 .B67 2023 (print) | LCC HQ767 (ebook) | DDC 362.1988/8082—dc23/eng/20230727
LC record available at https://lccn.loc.gov/2023022292
LC ebook record available at https://lccn.loc.gov/2023022293

Typeset in Fournier by Biblichor Ltd, Scotland
Printed and bound by CPI Group (UK) Ltd, Croydon, CR0 4YY

Contents

Introduction

We began learning in our practice to say, we don't need any doctors . . . We thought wow, that's amazing, we can do it ourselves, can't we? Without doctors . . . We began to realize that a well-performed abortion is never unsafe, what's unsafe is all those negative associations around it. (Guanajuato, Mexico)

I remember when, around 1999 or 2000, exciting news traveled through feminist networks about a new organization, Women on Waves—a Dutch doctor with a boat and crew who provided abortions in international waters offshore from countries with highly restrictive laws. At the time, I didn't know the details of how the abortions were done or how women got in touch with the boat when it was offshore, but it was the kind of creative and militant action that felt like a vicarious collective win for feminist health activists everywhere. I also did not know that fifteen years earlier women in Brazil had begun to use an ulcer medication to induce miscarriages, an early form of DIY medication abortion that reduced maternal mortality, and that information about this safer abortion strategy had spread across Latin America, where legal access to abortion was very limited.[1] These two strands of autonomous women's health activism would come together in 2008 in Ecuador when the members of Women on Waves trained a group of young feminists in Quito on the basics of medication abortion, leading to the launch of the Salud Mujeres abortion hotline, which still exists today. The Ecuadorian hotline, in turn, launched what has grown into a transnational feminist movement for self-managed medication abortion. While I (and many others) cheered on "the abortion boat" as it thumbed its nose at conservative politicians and their laws, it is the grassroots work that began in South America and spread globally that has changed countless women's lives, redefined the possibilities for having a safe abortion, and transformed the conversation in the United States post-*Dobbs*.

My real introduction to this movement started in the summer of 2015. National Advocates for Pregnant Women (now Pregnancy Justice) convened a daylong meeting that brought together activists from reproductive justice organizations and the early days of needle exchange to talk about what these movements might learn from each other, as access to abortion was becoming ever more restricted in the United States and medication abortion was replacing the "back alley" globally. I entered the room as a former needle exchange activist and left fascinated by the story of a medication that made illegal abortion relatively safe—and even more, the story of the women across the Global South who were teaching other women how to use it. This was a strategy, and a movement, that resonated deeply with my experience as an AIDS and harm-reduction activist in the 1990s as the war on drugs escalated and government at all levels abandoned people with or at risk for HIV.

Two years later, in June of 2017, I found myself outside the Bellas Artes metro station in downtown Santiago, Chile, in the late afternoon, waiting for a woman whose email I had gotten from an Ecuadorian who worked with an international NGO. At the time, the metro stations of Santiago were a common place to buy misoprostol—aka abortion pills. I paced around at the top of the metro stairs feeling simultaneously conspicuous and invisible in this small plaza filled with street vendors and students and colored by murals on the surrounding walls. After several minutes, a young woman came up to me, introduced herself, and then suggested we go to a tea shop around the corner. Over the next two years, I spent countless hours in cafés, tea shops, parks, shared apartments, and even a few NGO offices, exchanged more WhatsApp messages than I can count, and became familiar with encrypted communications platforms like Wire and Jitsi, as I learned about this global movement for reproductive justice that has shaped scientific knowledge and built new forms of solidarity while supporting people with unwanted pregnancies.

For about three years, from 2017 to 2019, I built relationships with self-managed medication abortion (SMA) activists in different parts of the world and learned about the work of the movement and the experiences of activists who are part of it. I traveled when I could, got to know people by email and other forms of internet-based communication, and eventually conducted recorded interviews with seventy people (sixty-nine women and one man) in addition to informal conversations with many more. I spent almost three months in Chile in 2017 and 2018, over three different trips, during a time period when Chilean abortion law first began to open up a little bit after the complete ban imposed by the military dictatorship of Augusto Pinochet in the 1980s. I visited Amsterdam three times during that period as well, and then in 2019 had an exhausting and energizing series of trips to Ecuador, Mexico, Nigeria, and Kenya before being abruptly grounded, like everyone else, in March of 2020. I probably did half of my interviews using online communications platforms, often building on relationships that began during or were facilitated by an in-person visit. There were three NGOs, including one of the online telehealth platforms, that made collective decisions to participate in the project, but otherwise my interviews were done with individual activists who chose to participate in the project rather than with organizations. I also became familiar with many websites and a wide range of digital materials, and worked with a student who followed the emerging public discourse about SMA in the United States on Twitter, Instagram, and TikTok for a few months in 2021. (Anyone interested in the formal, academic description of the methodology can find that in a paper published in 2022.[2])

By 2022, feminist activism to enable SMA had spread to at least thirty-three countries and four continents as activists had combined advocacy for decriminalization with pragmatic support for people who need a safe abortion now, regardless of the law. These are not separate groups that function in isolation but well-networked organizations doing similar work and engaged in ongoing regional and global conversations to share experience, knowledge, and mutual support. The first hotlines, for example, grew out of long-standing feminist organizations, and became autonomous collectives with a specific focus on direct action for SMA. In the Chilean city of Concepción, members of a feminist organization received an email about the new safe abortion hotline, Salud Mujeres, with a video of the events surrounding its official launch and were inspired to create their own hotline in Chile. Throughout Latin America, news of the hotline spread further through a feminist conference that dates back to the struggles against military dictatorships of the 1980s. The hotline network in Africa formalized existing connections among grassroots NGOs that were working on sexual and reproductive health and attending the same regional and international feminist health conferences. This is a feminist movement in the most concrete sense of the word, and is understood as such by the activists involved: there are regional networks, occasional global meetings, and shared action strategies.

It would be difficult to make sense of the relatively holistic nature of this work if you look at it as anything other than a movement, although from the outside—especially from the Global North—it may seem a little hard to pinpoint, going in and out of focus. As with other twenty-first-century movements, the movement for SMA is networked, horizontal, and dispersed, rather than centralized and hierarchical.[3] There is no analogue to Martin Luther King, SDS, ACT UP, or other iconic organizations and widely recognized leaders of past movements. The movement for SMA is largely low profile and has no central leadership. Women on Waves played a significant early role and still runs high-profile media-oriented campaigns, but only came up in my interviews with activists as part of the movement's origin story, or as one source of medication among others. There are important regional organizations, and vital centers of work: Las Socorristas are a network in Argentina notable for their size, relative visibility, and their combination of a sophisticated knowledge of SMA and a deeply radical feminist politics. But at the same time, they are a network of accompaniment collectives, like many others across the globe.

This lack of centralization is part of what makes it difficult, from the outside, to see the movement as an interconnected whole. Collectives form locally with a base in a pre-existing organization or feminist social network and contact more established collectives to learn how to set up a hotline or practice accompaniment, the activist work of supporting a person going through a self-managed abortion. This kind of dispersed, informal network is not unique, and has been described in social movement theory using the botanist's term "rhizomatic," for the way relatively invisible root networks connect local organizing across multiple locations, with each local group—each visible leaf, plant, or feminist collective—simultaneously organic to its place and linked to others across distance.[4] One recent example of this form of organizing is Black Lives Matter, another twenty-first-century movement, which emerged seemingly spontaneously as a horizontal, dispersed mass movement, without one formal leadership body, but which engaged in highly visible mass actions in major cities across the United States and around the world.

In addition, the movement for SMA and other similar movements such as needle exchange/harm reduction can be difficult to "see" precisely because the nature of their work demands a low profile under many circumstances. The phrase "social movement" conjures up demonstrations, sit-ins, blockades, and other forms of highly visible public confrontation, but the core definition of "civil disobedience" is not to get arrested in front of cameras but to refuse to follow an unjust law. In many circumstances, that refusal may need to be public in order to be effective, as in the burning of draft cards or the Freedom Riders who refused to comply with segregation on interstate transport—but the heart of civil disobedience lies in the refusal, not the publicity or the arrest.

The movement for SMA refuses to comply with laws that limit or ban abortion, and this work enables people with unwanted pregnancies to safely end those pregnancies regardless of the law. In effect, this is civil disobedience without a press release. The direct actions that support and enable SMA need to be visible enough to be accessible to people seeking help, and yet not so visible that they exacerbate fear or risk. This doesn't mean clandestinity, except when it is absolutely necessary, and most activists acknowledged that a certain level of visibility provided safety as well as reduced stigma. Collectives and individual activists attend demonstrations and engage in confrontational politics, but holding a workshop, answering a hotline, or accompanying someone through an abortion are not moments for highly visible, media-oriented confrontation. In a context of high stigma and criminalization, direct action to enable bodily autonomy and self-determination can be more powerful and effective precisely when it is relatively quiet and low profile.

At its most basic, direct action, as the phrase suggests, aims to directly interfere with or disrupt the "business as usual" of institutions as part of movements or struggles to bring about social change. Direct action typically focuses on institutions—blockades to stop gas pipelines, for example—but the direct action discussed in this book disrupts legal and institutional oppression through solidarity with and practical support for people facing criminalization. Direct action based in solidarity enacts a profound disruption of the institutional violence resulting from a law and/or a criminalized context. Accompanying someone through a self-managed abortion, especially in a context of legal restriction, may not be technically a violation of the law (although that depends on where you are and what exactly you do) but it is a profound disruption of institutional violence through the provision of support and care based in solidarity. Laws restricting abortion enact violence through denial of bodily autonomy, through social stigma linked to and combined with legal criminalization, and through the isolation that results from the convergence of these multiple forms of violence; the movement for SMA disrupts all of it by providing information and support to enable someone to reclaim their autonomy, and by standing with them so they are not isolated and alone through the process.

The structure of this kind of direct action looks very different than many other forms of political work since visibility is not the goal, and in fact would generally limit the effectiveness of the action. There are no signs, banners, or press releases in the moments and locations where the most crucial—and radical—forms of solidarity-based action take place. This goes against the intuitive structure of most social movement work, and almost all (other) forms of direct action that center visible, public acts of disruption. The public disruption of the movement for SMA lies in the visibility of its existence—the websites and phone numbers and more public workshops—not in the actual process which must remain invisible to everyone but those immediately involved. The movement demonstrates, on a daily basis, the impossibility of banning abortion and affirms the fundamental human right to bodily self-determination as well as the full humanity of persons facing marginalization and criminalization for exercising their right to self-determination.

This book explores a global movement that works across a wide range of social and historical contexts but does so through the lens of particular locations and experiences in parts of Latin America, sub-Saharan Africa, Europe, and the United States. Because each location has its own particular social, legal, and historical context, this book is necessarily exploratory and at times comparative rather than exhaustive. This is truly a global movement: comprehensive description of what is taking place everywhere would require a multivolume series. My aim is to offer a general picture of SMA as a transnational feminist movement, rather than go into the specifics of work in each organization or city. I focus on common patterns and histories, explorations of similarity and difference, that enable us to see how activists navigate the dynamics of unwanted pregnancies across particular social and historical locations.

For example, prior to 2020, abortion laws may have been generally more restrictive in Latin America than in sub-Saharan Africa, but the mortality rate from illegal abortions is much higher in Africa for reasons that have more to do with socioeconomic factors and medical systems than with laws per se.[5] In a slightly different example, before Argentina fully legalized abortion, Brazil and Argentina had very similar laws on abortion itself, but in Brazil other laws were used to target and criminalize activist strategies to support SMA whereas in Argentina activists could work much more openly.[6] The opportunities and constraints faced by activists emerge from the context as a whole, and not just from the technicalities of laws about abortion itself.

The book begins with brief histories of abortion and the emergence of activism for SMA, and a general introduction of the regions where I did research, before going into a more detailed exploration of different aspects of the work of the movement. Threaded through this will be some reflection on social movements and direct action, with occasional comparisons to other movements as useful. Chapter 1 will start with a brief overview of abortion law in the United States, the history likely to seem most immediately relevant to the majority of readers, and then explore the emergence of the movement for SMA. In chapter 2, I will return to historical and contextual concerns through an exploration of some key issues in each of the regions included in this book. The criminalization of abortion has roots in the professionalization of medicine in Europe and the United States, and in the colonial imposition of European laws in Latin America and sub-Saharan Africa; these histories may seem distant but are relevant to thinking about the radical potential of the movement for SMA to chart new pathways for all of us. The criminalization of abortion may have moved from the Global North to the Global South, but this movement has the potential to reverse that as feminist knowledge and practices around demedicalized, self-managed abortion move from the Global South to the Global North.

The middle section of the book, chapters 3 through 5, engage with the essential activist strategies and practices of the movement. The heart of this movement consists of a set of practical strategies for providing information and support, based in principles of solidarity and care, for people facing unwanted pregnancies. Chapter 3 explores the primary direct-action strategies that activists have developed, the ways these are implemented in the different places where I did research, and some of the lived experiences of actually doing this work in a day-to-day way. Chapter 4 goes into the risks associated with these forms of direct action, and the security practices that have developed over time that enable activists—and people seeking abortions—to manage those risks. Right-wing movements shape the risks, political and otherwise, faced by reproductive justice activists and people seeking abortions, and chapter 4 includes a brief examination of the role of global far-right networks in the political environments within which activists work. Chapter 5 explores activist engagement with research and science, another set of movement practices that both grow out of and enable direct action to support SMA. A considerable amount of the scientific literature on self-managed medication abortion, as opposed to clinic-based medication abortion, has been done through ongoing partnerships between activist organizations and epidemiologists.

The last two chapters step back from the focus on strategies and practices to take a slightly larger perspective on how the movement does its work, and the experience of the long-term activists who have built and sustained it. Chapter 6 describes the networks among organizations and individuals that support the development of new collectives and the exchange of knowledge and experience, and that fundamentally underlie activists' experience of their work as part of a transnational feminist movement. The activists I spoke with in each particular location had ties to other collectives within their country, but also knew that they were part of a web of interconnected organizations regionally and globally. Where chapter 6 looks at geographic interconnections, chapter 7 takes the long view on how a commitment to activism, and specifically to direct action for SMA, both emerges from and comes to shape the lives of activists. Any thriving organization includes people who have been involved for varying periods of time, from the newest members through the original founders; the majority of the people I interviewed had been involved for many years, and chapter 7 explores their experience from initial engagement through the time of the interview. The conclusion aspires to bring together the diverse threads that run through the book, offer some final thoughts on social movements and direct action, and consider how all this may be useful moving forward.

~

It is important to recognize that SMA is not the only movement that engages in solidarity-based direct actions around health that build from a larger social justice framework. A few years ago, I wrote an essay about autonomous health movements based on SMA and my own prior experience with harm reduction in relation to drug use and HIV, and it seems useful to lay out the core framework here.[7]

Autonomous health movements (AHMs) have a few key characteristics: they emerge from larger social justice movements to address stigmatized and/or criminalized health issues that affect their population/constituency, they engage in direct action that involves the demedicalization of knowledge and/or technology previously controlled by medical institutions, and they are willing to work at the margins of the law when necessary. For example, the movement for SMA emerged within a larger feminist movement in contexts where abortion was highly restricted, it has adapted medication protocols for safe and effective use within ordinary community settings, and it has been willing to do work that not infrequently falls into a gray area of the law. Similarly, syringe exchange programs and overdose prevention emerged within a larger social justice struggle during the HIV/AIDS epidemic in order to get sterile injection equipment and naloxone to drug users, often in defiance of the law, and thereby enable criminalized drug users to become effective public health activists. The health education and support done by sex worker–activists in many parts of the world is intrinsically at the margins of the law given the criminalization of sex work, and is frequently informed by a strong feminist perspective on labor and sexual rights. There are other examples across the world at varying levels of visibility. Each of these movements engages in solidarity-based direct action to enable bodily autonomy and self-determination within marginalized, criminalized contexts through a combination of practical support and collective care that actively disrupts societal stigmatization and isolation.

Movements sometimes struggle to identify their victories, but the direct-action strategies created by AHMs can change public health practices and health care in significant ways. The movement for SMA has reduced maternal mortality statistics globally and, as will be discussed in more detail in chapter 5, reshaped the World Health Organization's protocols for medication abortion and even their classification of abortions from a safe/unsafe binary into a spectrum of safety and risk.[8] The importance of this can be seen in the immediate post-*Dobbs* emphasis on access to abortion medication, and whether this can be maintained through FDA authority even in states that ban abortion. These conversations assume the safety of SMA as the basis around which some level of access could be upheld, a perspective that only exists because of the work of this movement and its affiliated scientists.

As another example, in much of the United States, syringe exchange began as illegal direct action that was gradually legalized. In NYC, where rates of HIV among drug users were around 50 percent in the 1980s, there were significant declines in HIV seroprevalence among injection drug users in NYC five years after programs began working at multiple locations, and rates have continued to drop to the point where drug injection is no longer a significant risk factor for HIV in the city.[9] In India, sex worker organizations transformed the response to HIV prevention and health care through direct action and community organizing in profoundly marginalized contexts—creating model strategies later promoted by global health institutions like the WHO.

It is important to recognize that these new models for care began with social movements working at the margins of the law. Throughout the book, I will occasionally draw parallels to other movements and forms of direct action that share characteristics with SMA because seeing connections across movements can help us think creatively about how knowledge can be developed, used, and shared.

The majority of this book centers the Global South and transnational activism, yet at the same time, I assume that the primary readership of this book will be in North America during a time of profound political struggle around reproductive justice and bodily autonomy. These two factors shape how material is introduced and presented in various ways. At times, I begin or end a chapter with a US-oriented perspective to connect the material to its North American readers. For example, chapter 1 begins with a brief history of abortion law in the United States, leading to our current situation, while the history of abortion law as a product of European colonialism in Latin America and sub-Saharan Africa does not appear until chapter 2 as part of the exploration of regional patterns. In addition, I try not to assume that the people reading this book have traveled widely, and do my best to make the places and people at the heart of this project come alive in a way that will be accessible to someone whose travels are more intellectual than physical. This is a transnational movement, which includes the United States (where "abortion" and "pills" are linked ever more frequently), and those of us in the United States have a lot to learn from our *compañeras* in the Global South. For some this is already reflexive—I was not the only person who carried *un pañuelo verde* (a green bandana) from Latin America in the streets of NYC on the night the *Dobbs* decision was formally released—but hopefully this book can help bring US activists into deeper (and more humble) dialogue with feminists beyond our borders. We have a lot to learn in a world of shared struggle. *Adelante*.

1

Abortion Is Unstoppable: The Emergence of a Transnational Movement

> *I think that a big part of this movement is . . . the way it's a women's politics, joining together to solve everyday problems among ourselves . . . For many of the sectors who rule this world, we're committing an offense. And so, on this sometimes slippery ledge we're moving along, I think we're also developing a particular kind of feminism . . . A feminism of direct action, body to body.* (Argentina)

When the US Supreme Court overturned *Roe v Wade*, they upended a way of organizing medical care—and life—that women of reproductive age in the United States largely took for granted. In June 2022, when the *Dobbs* decision was officially released, abortion had been legal for forty-nine years, and while it had been increasingly difficult to access in much of the United States, there is a vast difference between "inaccessible" and "illegal." In states that have banned abortion, doctors (and hospital lawyers) calculate the odds of criminal prosecution and even incarceration as they make decisions about care for pregnant women with health conditions, often critical ones, that are incompatible with continuing a pregnancy. In states like Texas, where support for a person seeking an abortion has been criminalized, abortion funds have scrambled to figure out whether they can still operate and, in many cases, have had to close their doors and/or relocate to a different state.

In the two months between the leak of *Dobbs* and its official publication, abortion supporters chanted, "We will not go back!" And they were right, despite the ruling: the reality is that we have not gone back to 1972, a time before both abortion pills and the antiabortion movement. Instead, we have gone forward into a time in which abortion can be done safely outside the medical system, and increasingly violent far-right movements use gender and sexuality to recruit and mobilize in the United States and globally.

The dominant American experience of abortion as a medical procedure that takes place in a women's health clinic has become normalized, but historically it's a very recent invention. Until the mid-nineteenth century, there was no meaningful boundary between irregular menstruation and pregnancy prior to "quickening," when a fetus begins to move inside the womb, and the practical management of reproduction was the responsibility of women, midwives, and other informal healers within a community.[1] As a result, abortion was largely not criminalized in the United States, especially in the first four to five months of pregnancy before the fetus begins to move.[2] The creation of "abortion" as a medical event in need of professional intervention was part of the formalization, and masculinization, of the practice of medicine in the United States, England, and Europe.[3] As medicine professionalized, the risks from abortion in the late 1800s were used as one part of a strategy to draw boundaries between "doctors" and "quacks."[4] This social relocation of abortion from a largely informal and unregulated practice handled by women into a medicalized process handled by male professionals also brought abortion into criminal law: by 1900, all US states had banned abortion except under a narrow range of conditions.[5] Interestingly, during this time Catholic and Protestant churches were relatively indifferent to the issue; the primary opposition came from the new American Medical Association, who condemned abortion, even by doctors, under virtually all circumstances other than to save the life of the mother.[6] The AMA's opposition to abortion reflected concerns over health and an emerging understanding of fetal development, as well as the assertion of professional boundaries, but in the process male doctors began to conceptually separate the fetus from the life of a pregnant woman.

Abortion became a visible social issue again in the 1960s, and the clinics and women's health centers that are now the iconic (and embattled) locations for abortion services in the United States began as a feminist project in the early and mid-1970s.[7] Feminist activists conducted visible and confrontational campaigns to legalize abortion, expand access to contraception for those who wanted it, and transform women's experiences of health care. There were protests in the streets, at medical conferences, and in courts; sit-ins in hospitals and legislative offices; and relentless campaigns to change laws and expand access to birth control and abortion.[8] In addition, and less visibly, feminist organizations engaged in pragmatic direct action to assist women with abortion, moving information that had previously circulated secretly within private networks into public form.[9] In California, activists not only compiled a list of known abortionists in Mexico near the US border, but also gathered service reviews from women who had gone to those doctors and, when necessary, would pressure a doctor to improve his practices or be removed from the list.[10] An activist collective in Boston created a self-help course to help women learn about their bodies, including ways to end an early-stage pregnancy, and their resource manual eventually became the widely available book, *Our Bodies, Ourselves*.[11] The Los Angeles Women's Health Center created programs they called "self-help clinics," where a group of women would meet for a number of weeks to learn gynecological self-examination and "demystify" their bodies using kits, pamphlets, and other materials that circulated widely in the United States and Canada.[12]

When abortion was legalized, first in states like New York and California and then federally through the 1973 *Roe* decision, women's health clinics and abortion clinics emerged to provide the newly legal service. These clinics were founded by women's health activists and allied doctors to intentionally create an environment that went against the dominant hierarchical structures of medical care.[13] While freestanding clinics enabled the development of woman-centered and explicitly feminist models of care, they also reinforced the separation and isolation of abortion from regular gynecological and primary care.[14] It is worth emphasizing that there is no medical reason for this approach, and abortion could easily be integrated with primary care, as is more common in other parts of the world.[15]

It is important to recognize the role of the far right in the structure of abortion care in the United States, and to understand why abortion care is so embattled and so isolated from other health services. In 1973, when *Roe* was decided, right-wing organizing focused on defending segregation more than traditional gender roles, and even the Southern Baptist Convention passed resolutions in 1971, '74, and '76 supporting legal access to abortion under a range of conditions.[16] In the late 1970s, there was a deliberate shift in the focus of right-wing organizing away from segregation and towards gender/sexuality issues, a shift that has come to shape religious beliefs as well as women's access to medical care.[17] The previously supportive and empowering care environment of "women's health" services became embattled and isolated by the systematic political (and physical) assaults of the antiabortion far right, which made abortion care literally a dangerous profession. Abortion providers and clinics across the United States have been subject to shootings, arson, bombings, and countless threats since the emergence of an antiabortion movement in the late 1970s.

From 1993 to 2016, far-right activists have murdered eleven people at abortion clinics and (unsuccessfully) attempted to kill twenty-six others.[18] It's one thing to offer a stigmatized service within a multiservice community care clinic, but quite another to provide one that is the target of politically motivated violence that could place staff and patients at risk.

On the surface, the *Dobbs* decision appears to replicate the pre-*Roe* situation by giving states the ability to regulate abortion, but, as noted earlier, the social and political terrain are profoundly different now than in the early 1970s. There is no going back to pre-*Roe* socially, medically, or politically, and to frame *Dobbs* as doing so reflects right-wing aspirations to return to a former world in which White men and the heterosexual nuclear family held hegemonic power. The Center for Reproductive Rights and the Guttmacher Institute maintain constantly updated maps of abortion laws at the state level that clearly show how much access to abortion has declined even relative to 2021. Under *Roe,* the major cities within conservative states often provided some protection for those who lived nearby or could travel; under *Dobbs*, service provision is determined at the state level, and given the political map of the United States there are now entire regions in which the majority of states have restricted or banned abortion. While spatially this may have some resemblance to the pre-*Roe* map of state laws, the depth of politicization has changed the level of criminalization, fear, and uncertainty for everyone involved. Another key difference today, of course, is the ability to have a genuinely safe self-managed abortion outside the medical system using a handful of pills and instructions that can easily fit on one page.

Self-managed abortion emerges from new technologies while building on previous feminist strategies to enable women to safely end pregnancies outside the medical system. The most direct predecessor to twenty-first-century SMA was the Jane Collective in

Chicago, a direct action group that formed in the late 1960s to provide abortions to any woman who needed one, and who continued their work until the 1973 *Roe* decision.[19] Jane initially connected women to a man who claimed to be a doctor, but when they found out he wasn't one they quickly learned how to do it themselves and began to operate their own abortion service out of a series of Chicago apartments.[20] In a twenty-first-century parallel, a group of feminists in Mexico brought women to a local gynecologist but over time, by listening to the doctor's instructions, they learned how to safely do a medication abortion. One of the key similarities to contemporary SMA collectives is that Jane provided abortions to anyone, regardless of their politics or ability to pay, and there was no requirement to join an ongoing self-help group or otherwise join the movement. This set Jane apart from other feminist health collectives that were ongoing groups within which women learned about their own bodies and sometimes engaged in practices like menstrual extraction, which enabled safe abortions for early-stage pregnancies, but also required specialized equipment plus some training and experience to be done safely and effectively.[21] Jane worked to make abortions available to anyone who called their phone number seeking help.

In the early 1970s, there was no safe, reliable, easily taught method through which a woman could directly abort her own pregnancy, but towards the end of the twentieth century, new medications opened up fundamentally new possibilities. The standard medical protocol for medication abortion involves two drugs, mifepristone and misoprostol, which are taken in sequence: mifepristone is taken first to block a hormone needed to maintain a pregnancy and to help the cervix open, and then misoprostol is used to induce uterine contractions.[22] Mifepristone is an abortion medication, while misoprostol was first created to treat gastric ulcers and has many medical uses, including the prevention of postpartum hemorrhage. The two-drug combination was introduced in

France in the late 1980s, and then spread through Europe before finally being authorized in the United States in 2000. Around the time medication abortion began in France, women in Brazil started to use misoprostol, under the brand name Cytotec, to induce abortions outside the medical system under conditions of extremely limited legal access.[23] While there is no "origin story" of the first woman to take misoprostol alone as an abortifacient, the medication was widely available in pharmacies throughout Latin America as an ulcer treatment and came with a visible warning label on the package stating that pregnant women should not use the drug as it could cause a miscarriage; it does not require much imagination to read the warning label as an invitation. Misoprostol, if allowed to dissolve under the tongue, has the added benefit of being undetectable when uterine contractions begin, making it impossible to prove whether a miscarriage is induced or spontaneous, keeping its user safer in relation to legal persecution.

These two approaches to medication abortion are widely used today, with the two-drug combination available through doctors and online telemedicine services, and misoprostol alone used as a more accessible strategy in many different circumstances. Unsurprisingly, there are thriving black markets for combination packs of mifepristone (Mife) and misoprostol (Miso) and for Miso alone. When the US-based organization Plan C tested samples from a range of online sources in 2016–17, they found that all were of high enough quality to induce an abortion.[24] In 2012 the WHO included self-managed abortion in its technical and policy guidance for abortion but reserved the language of "safe" only for abortion with medical supervision; more recently, the WHO has shifted to a spectrum of safety and risk, recognizing abortions outside the medical system as more and less safe depending on method and circumstances.[25] There is a growing body of epidemiological research demonstrating that SMA can be as safe when performed entirely in the community as it is when it starts in a doctor's office or clinic.[26] Much of the research on SMA has been done in conjunction with activist hotlines and other SMA support collectives in Latin America, Africa, and Indonesia (discussed in chapter 5 on the science of SMA), providing peer-reviewed scientific evidence of the safety, efficacy, and power of the work of this transnational feminist movement based on demedicalization, autonomy, and solidarity.

Organized feminist action for SMA began in the early 2000s in Europe with the Women on Waves boat campaigns, and a few years later the creation of the first telemedicine platform, Women on Web. Women on Waves (Waves) and Women on Web (Web) are related organizations; Waves conducts visibility-oriented campaigns in countries that have highly restrictive abortion laws, while Web is a telemedicine platform that provides online abortion care. Waves began in 1999/2000 and the Web platform came online around 2006, although email communication with women seeking abortions began before Web was officially launched. The Web platform became the basic template for other online telemedicine abortion services, combining a simple interface with a complex behind-the-scenes structure. People seeking abortions fill out an online consultation form, communicate by email with a multilingual "help desk," and, if appropriate, receive abortion pills sent by mail. Emails are managed through a central system, sorted by language, such that members of a "language team" (e.g. Spanish, Polish, Portuguese) log in to the system during designated shifts to respond to whatever emails have come in to their group (more on this in chapter 3).

The formal structure that underlies the international telemedicine platforms is complex and spread out over multiple countries for legal reasons. As described by women who worked for Web in its early days, the apparently singular entity actually consisted of two linked NGOs, each of which was registered in a different country based on who had the most liberal laws around particular issues, plus a doctor licensed independently in a third country. One NGO was registered in Canada, where abortion is fully decriminalized and online pharmacy laws are relatively liberal. The financial entity was registered in the Netherlands and manages all aspects of donations, grants, salaries, and expenses. The doctors have been licensed in Moldova or Austria, both of which have particularly liberal laws around the online prescription of abortion medications. Medications are then shipped from India, where the majority of the globe's generic medication is produced. (This in turn created a global medication crisis when Indian airports were closed in response to the COVID pandemic). This basic structure enabled the platform to maximize the legal strengths of different countries while evading areas of greater restriction, and to create a system that could legally send abortion medication to women in most of the world.

The basic Web model has since been adapted by other online abortion telemedicine platforms that do international work. The United States may be the only country with the dubious distinction of threatening one of the international abortion platforms with legal action over the shipping of medication: in March 2019, Aid Access, the US-oriented platform associated with Web, received a threatening letter from the FDA regarding "misbranded and unapproved drugs." Nonetheless, they have continued to ship abortion pills to women in the United States without further consequences. And the US mail service does not appear to intercept Aid Access packages, unlike some other countries that have not legally challenged the telemedicine platforms but will identify and destroy individual medication packs.

While Waves' abortion boat conducted highly visible campaigns in a number of countries, the one in Portugal proved to be indirectly significant to the emergence of a larger movement. In 2004, Waves and a group of Portuguese feminists organized a campaign that included a visit by the abortion boat to a Portuguese port. A hotline was set up so that women who wanted an abortion could contact activists and the ship. All of this was ordinary procedure, but when Waves arrived the Portuguese Navy sent two military ships to "meet" the Waves boat and prevent it from entering the port. The warships continued to "guard" the Waves boat as it remained in international waters for almost two weeks. In response, Waves published the medical protocol for the use of misoprostol online, and Portuguese activists learned the protocol and shared it with women who called the hotline.

After the Waves boat returned to the Netherlands, the hotline continued until 2007, when abortion through the tenth week was legalized within the Portuguese medical system. The decision to continue the hotline after the departure of the Waves boat was the moment when the Portuguese campaign crossed over into new territory. Initially, the hotline was a shared project among several activists but was maintained for almost three years by a woman who later joined the staff of Web. She insisted that it wasn't very difficult, as there were only about thirty calls per month and the hotline number was only advertised on the Waves/Web site. But this was the first time that an SMA hotline had functioned independently, even on a small scale, and it prefigured the autonomous hotlines that have since spread throughout the world. Importantly, the woman who kept answering the Portuguese hotline from 2004 until the law changed in 2007 was part of the Web staff who supported the launch of the Ecuadorian hotline in 2008—which was the beginning of a transnational strategy for self-managed medication abortion.

The Ecuadorian hotline that emerged in 2008 began as a Waves campaign in which, once again, the boat ran into some problems and an alternative plan had to be created on the fly. As a former boat captain described,

> The boat crashed . . . So, we had to think of another option when we were sitting in the plane on our way to Ecuador . . . We saw in the

> booklets, the tourist guide. We saw this big statue. So, that was what we proposed to the Ecuadorian women . . . We were from the old feminist generation who still made banners.

As a result, the boat campaign was transformed into the launch of the new hotline, and a banner with the phone number was dropped from an enormous statue of the Virgin Mary in Quito. Unlike in Portugal, however, the hotline in Ecuador, Salud Mujeres, was designed by a collective to be a long-term autonomous project, and it set in motion a regional strategy that subsequently spread to other continents. Staff from Web trained the hotline collective in protocols for medication abortion with Mife and Miso and with Miso alone so that they could teach hotline callers how to safely self-manage a medication abortion. At that time, Miso was relatively available in Ecuadorian pharmacies, although this began to change as knowledge about SMA spread and the government began to reduce community-level access, which has been a fairly common response globally to increased visibility of SMA.

The Ecuadorian feminists were experienced activists who were well integrated into national and regional networks, and word of the first hotline spread rapidly among feminist organizations in South America. A woman who was part of the original hotline in Chile said,

> We heard of the experience of Women on Waves and their connection with Ecuador, and they reached out to us, you know? With this email network and everything, we received a video of the launch of the hotline in Ecuador, in which they climb up the Virgin's statue [in Quito] . . . We started discussing and making contact; the most experienced group, the Bio Bio feminists, got in touch with our compañeras in Ecuador . . . They were in talks, and we assembled a group of women who were sure of wanting to go ahead with the project and give it a local focus.

Within two to three years, there were hotlines in Argentina, Chile, and Peru, and others soon followed as activists studied available medical information, got trained by those with more experience, and shared hotline protocols, challenges, and publicity strategies with each other.

Medication abortion was the obvious technological innovation underlying the rapidly developing movement for SMA, but cellphones and the internet were central to the movement's operations and strategies. Hotlines generally were (and still are) cellphones circulated among collective members who share the responsibility for answering; and launch videos, medication protocols, and unanticipated problems were all shared via email through regional networks and with Web. In addition, there are many websites with instructions on the use of medication, hotline manuals produced in multiple languages, videos, zines, and, of course, a growing number of telemedicine sites.

A few years before the Ecuadorian hotline was launched, feminists in Mexico initiated a somewhat different abortion education and support strategy known as "*acompañamiento*" or "accompaniment." Accompaniment as an activist strategy is simultaneously as simple and as complicated as the word suggests: a trained activist will accompany someone through an abortion, staying with them physically or being in regular contact by phone or text message as the abortion progresses, offering support as needed, both emotionally and informationally (e.g. how much bleeding is normal). This practice is part of long-standing feminist work across Latin America, as feminists engage in *acompañamiento* around rape, domestic violence, and the aftermath of *feminicidio* (femicide) as well as abortion, supporting individuals and families through the medical and legal aftermath of different forms of violence against women.

In the early 2000s, a feminist human rights organization in Guanajuato, a conservative state in central Mexico, developed abortion accompaniment as part of their work with rape survivors. At the time, rape was one of the only legal grounds for abortion in Guanajuato and when the state tried to eliminate even that option, activists fought back. They were able to maintain legal access for rape survivors, and in the process began to accompany survivors first through connections with local gynecologists and later through learning how to do medication abortions themselves. The director of the organization described how she began to learn the protocol:

> One of the gynecologists came back one day from a gynecology and obstetrics congress . . . She said to me, you know what? There's this pill that induces an abortion . . . You can buy it at the pharmacy . . . And so I watched how she handled the whole abortion process for various women with pills . . . And when I learned, she never knew what she'd done, right? She didn't know she'd taught me.

In 2007, abortion was legalized in Mexico City and an NGO there began to accompany women coming to the city for abortions by helping them navigate the process, while also offering web-based information and support to women in other parts of the country who needed an abortion but could not travel. I have no doubt that throughout the world there are other stories about the emergence of DIY medication abortion and support in the mid-2000s or earlier, stories of individuals or groups that did what they could with varying levels of information, organization, desperation, and liberation.

The public-facing campaigns of Waves were (and are) designed to draw media attention, but starting in 2008 the staff of Web quietly trained local activists in medication abortion in Latin America, Africa, and anywhere else there was a group interested in being trained. The campaigns organized through Waves had long included teaching local partner organizations as well as individual women about medication abortion, but the launch of the Ecuadorian hotline led to a new pathway, separate from Waves campaigns, for Web staff to train activists in what came to be called self-managed abortion. In 2009 and 2010, Web staff and members of the Ecuadorian hotline collective worked together to train activists in Argentina and Chile in medication abortion and hotline procedures. Former Web staff described doing trainings on medication abortion in Indonesia, Tanzania, Thailand, and other countries throughout the early 2010s, and some of those women did similar trainings in the United States, particularly in the southern states, during the Trump administration.

The high-profile media-oriented campaigns of Waves involved very different kinds of work from the long-term international relationships being built by some of the Web staff, and the level of interconnection between the two organizations made it difficult to develop both approaches simultaneously. These tensions ultimately led to the formation of a new organization built around a different model of transnational work.

In 2014, the staff of Web collectively split off to create a separate organization, Women Help Women (WHW), designed to continue the work they had begun within Web to demedicalize SMA and enhance the focus on long-term relationships with local partners. One of the women involved in this transition described the shift in the following way:

> The main change was a real need to demedicalize and to really spread its possibilities and not being so focused on a service that is working somewhere in the world but is not locally involved . . . [This approach is] more creative in the sense that we are doing more training—local trainings. We are providing medicine where it is not available, and are less focused on countries where misoprostol is more easily available. But we are working everywhere: in Africa, in Asia, in South America, in so many different contexts.

The development of long-term, ongoing partnerships built on shared work is a different model of relationship than high-profile, short-term, location-specific campaigns, and this is especially true in transnational Global North/Global South collaborations. While Waves and Web are formally separate, in practice they represent different expressions of the vision of the doctor who founded and continues to be centrally involved in both. (Aid Access is a third arm of this linked group.) The former Web staff members who created WHW described their decision as driven by multiple concerns, but a central one was their experience of not having the space to develop ongoing, horizontal, collaborative partnerships with local activists in Latin America and Africa. The activist quoted above went on to say,

> [Leaving] made us also be more radical. We had less to lose, maybe, and could say, "Well, let's really try to change—to think what we can change" . . . It involves dreaming, but also knowing that you cannot be just a shadow of Women on Web. You have to be something different.

These women built an organization that is much lower profile, at least outside the network of international abortion organizations, and does not make media-oriented campaigns a central part of their work. WHW operates a telehealth platform that prescribes and sends medication to people with unwanted pregnancies, and also builds ongoing partnerships with community-based SMA organizations in much of the world. In doing so, the group brings core principles of direct action based in solidarity and care into a transnational context that combines direct support to individuals with participation in organizational networks involved in training, access to medication and other resources, and support for new initiatives, among other things. In 2018, for example, I attended an "information share" on abortion pills in Bushwick, Brooklyn, led by someone who works for Women Help Women and had been a former Web intern, as part of a series of events on women's health hosted by a local community-based organization.

This short history of the emergence of SMA highlights some themes that are present throughout the movement and this book. First, certain kinds of direct action require a low profile rather than a media-oriented public confrontation, and this is a lasting difference between Waves/Web and WHW as well as a key element of work on hotlines. This extends to organizational partnerships and networks, which focus on shared work over the long term rather than short-term campaigns. Another key difference—one that WHW shares with the hotlines, accompaniment, and other SMA direct-action groups globally—is that they are not led by a medical professional, and almost none of the members of the organization have formal medical training. WHW runs an online telemedicine service, and the team includes a doctor who prescribes medication for the service, but she is another member of the online team. This is a very different organizational and sociopolitical perspective than Waves and Web, which were founded and continue to be led by a (high-profile) doctor. It can be useful, even powerful, to have a doctor say that women can safely use abortion pills without medical supervision, but this still maintains the primacy of medical authority. Only people without formal medical training can truly demedicalize a process and bring it into community control, which is an essential aspect of SMA as a transnational feminist movement.

Another central element of the movement is its strong base in the Global South. While the international telemedicine platforms have played a crucial role in the initial development and ongoing work of the movement, the community-based direct action at the heart of the movement is centered in the Global South, as will become clear throughout this book. Even more, the direct-action strategies for supporting and enabling SMA in community settings have largely been developed in the Global South, not the Global North. There has been something of a division of labor, in which the North provides technical assistance in important moments, such as training in medication abortion and digital security, and activists in Latin America or Africa then adapt this information for their local environments and spread it within regional networks. This is important not just in terms of thinking about transnational (and decolonial) flows of information and knowledge, but because it has shaped the movement politically. The strategies developed by community-based activists for sharing information on SMA and supporting people through the abortion process place the experiences and needs of pregnant people at the center, and build demedicalized, community-based approaches to abortion. This is not abortion as a medical process, no matter how feminist: it is abortion as radical bodily autonomy and as ordinary life, simultaneously, "at home, with friends" to paraphrase the name of a Chilean collective.

Why is this community-based politics important? The movement largely emerged at the margins of the law, in contexts where access to abortion is highly restricted and most often criminalized, but the direct-action strategies themselves go beyond mere survival and prefigure new options for the future. This can be seen in Argentina, where SMA activists were deeply involved in the struggle to legalize abortion, which succeeded in 2020 when a new law made abortion legal without restrictions up to fourteen weeks. The accompaniment collectives throughout Argentina now continue their work with community-based SMA in this new legal context, charting new ground for the movement as a whole while also working with allies in the medical system to improve care in clinics and hospitals.

SMA is a feminist approach to managing reproduction in autonomous, community settings, not a provisional option only for use in legally restrictive contexts. This means that the demedicalized approaches created by activists will shape our understanding of abortion going forward. For example, in the United States, when abortion telemedicine was first broadly authorized under COVID, the new platforms initially tried to replicate the clinic experience online with video consultations, but quickly shifted to the asynchronous model of the international platforms like WHW, Web and AidAccess—largely in response to user/client preferences. The emergence of SMA as a community-based practice has already begun to shift institutional practices and will continue to shape our understandings of abortion in the future as demedicalization leads to deinstitutionalization.

There is much that we can learn from the transnational feminist movement for SMA in this ongoing period of technological change, social instability and upheaval, growing right-wing movements, and increasing progressive power. Times of instability are inherently times of change, and transformation begins at the margins rather than the center. In the 1960s and '70s, new technologies like manual vacuum aspiration and its feminist cousin menstrual extraction led to significant changes within and outside of the medical system. As abortion was legalized, first in the states and then federally, activists who had been doing direct action outside the system became involved in the creation of clinics that challenged traditional medicine and brought feminist practices into these new medical settings.[27] Medication abortion and digital communications, technological changes of the twenty-first century, have again transformed abortion both within and outside the medical system, and feminist SMA activists are at the forefront of creating new, less institutional ways to have an abortion. As the movement for SMA demonstrates every day, the question is not whether to fight for policy change or to help women directly; it is possible and necessary to do both, although at times through different organizations. Most importantly, the movement shows that direct action with people seeking abortions enables a reimagination of what abortion can be when it is liberated from the institutional structures of the medical system.

In social movement theory, direct action for SMA is a form of prefigurative action, meaning that it creates in the present some aspect of the society the movement works to build for the future. The "beloved community" of the Southern Civil Rights movement in the United States was prefigurative in its commitment to create truly multiracial communities of activists living and working together, as were the radically open decision-making processes in the Occupy movement in 2011. Accompaniment collectives in particular work to build alternative, prefigurative forms of supported autonomy and care for people who need abortions, and in a growing number of countries in Latin America this work continues under conditions of legality.[28] The institutional violence of medical systems goes much deeper than the regulation of abortion, and legal abortion can still be performed under conditions of marginalization and lack of respect for the bodily autonomy of the pregnant person. In general, direct action based on solidarity and care is intrinsically prefigurative, as activists and people seeking assistance work together to imagine and create forms of support based in mutual recognition, care, and an understanding of the deeply collective nature of autonomy and self-determination.

This work offers pathways for those of us living in the United States to fully engage with a struggle for justice, following the lead of African Americans and other women of color in the United States who have long demanded that we move beyond the narrow confines of "choice." Like most policies or court decisions, *Roe* has been simultaneously vital and limited, creating a right to abortion based in a right to privacy rather than a broader conception of women's rights and bodily autonomy. It also left abortion within the criminal code, which has had and will continue to have profound consequences for those who do not have access to the medical system—or privacy—for any number of reasons. SMA challenges, or invites, us to work for across-the-board decriminalization, the path taken by the Mexican Supreme Court in 2021, which would take abortion completely out of the criminal justice system. The criminal and court systems frame human action through a punitive lens by definition, and are deeply embedded in upholding structural systems of colonialism, racism, sexism, classism, heterosexism, and gender enforcement writ large (to choose only the most obviously relevant). Reproductive justice and bodily autonomy cannot be maintained through systems whose structures were designed to further marginalize people by framing their actions through the lens of potential criminality. The overturning of *Roe* has been and will continue to be devastating for countless people, but an effective response requires a larger framework than choice or privacy, and the closing of one door may force us to fight for the creation of other, more spacious, pathways forward.

A movement that has built strategies to enable the health and autonomy of those facing unwanted pregnancies under conditions of criminalization offers a vision of the possible, of what can happen when human needs take precedence over institutional needs. The majority of the activists who participated in this project were outside the United States and understand their work as part of ongoing feminist human rights struggles. In the United States, this commitment to a holistic analysis of reproduction is more likely to be articulated as reproductive justice, a perspective that emerged from African American women to reflect their historical experience of a multilayered loss of reproductive autonomy, including involuntary sterilization and the deliberate destruction of African American and Native American families. Human rights frameworks are powerful in postcolonial and postdictatorship societies, and asserting women's reproductive and bodily autonomy as human rights locates them within larger societal struggles for social and economic justice in a way that is analogous to reproductive justice frameworks in the United States.[29]

Regardless of the language used, the movement for SMA embodies the frameworks and spirit of reproductive justice through the use of direct actions that center solidarity and care as organizing principles. Movement strategies recognize the diverse circumstances that lead women to seek an abortion, and intentionally disrupt isolation and stigma while providing information and support for safe self-managed abortions. These strategies reflect a holistic understanding of the complexities of reproductive *in*justice that underlie both reproductive justice and human rights frameworks, even when abortion itself is the exclusive focus of action.

SMA intrinsically addresses a pregnancy and its ending within the context of a person's life, from the planning of how to manage the process around the other elements of day-to-day life to the experience of taking pills to end a pregnancy within a home or another personal space. Activists describe the ways they encounter, and emotionally or even physically enter, the life of the person who contacts an SMA collective as they accompany that person through the barriers, the planning, and often the abortion itself over hours or days. This is, in a very real way, a practice of solidarity rather than service, of mutuality rather than hierarchy. Chapter 3 will explore the different strategies activists have developed to educate, assist, and accompany women through the abortion process, to navigate the place of a particular pregnancy within a person's life, and to increase access overall to reproductive knowledge and bodily autonomy.

Across contexts and strategies, the heart of the movement for SMA is an embodied solidarity of recognition, accompaniment, and shared risk in the face of stigma and criminalization. The movement stands on a legal right to share information, and has built systems of shared trust and solidarity around that potentially narrow legal ground for action. Like the Jane Collective in the 1960s and '70s, SMA activists will help pregnant people who contact them regardless of whether or not that person is a feminist or an activist, simply because the person needs to not be pregnant. Activists talk about being drawn to SMA precisely because of the emphasis on solidarity-based direct action; for example, an activist in Ecuador from a working-class family who attended university while living with her mother in *un barrio popular* described how important it was to be part of a feminist collective that focused on helping ordinary women rather than debating theory.

> I guess that's what still keeps me in the collective. The way we've proceeded, always using direct action. It was never like that before with the feminism I knew. It's about practice, not theory.

The movement is built on a dual commitment to practical action that enables bodily autonomy and to accompaniment, to being with someone through a process. In the words of an Argentinian activist,

> It seems to me that what's so hopeful about the accompaniment movement lies partly in our certainty that this movement saves lives, takes care of people, and . . . [in how] we do politics to solve problems in the here and now, but without neglecting to think about more profound strategies for change.

2

We Are Everywhere: The Shape of the Global Movement for SMA

[We are] focused on the autonomy of women. Women should know that the decision is theirs, that we're going to support other women in their journey to the interruption of pregnancy, and what's more there are safe ways to achieve this while being accompanied.

Our understanding is that a self-administered abortion is not only an autonomous, self-caring decision, but also a decision of love—love for yourself . . . love for a society that could be, like, freer . . . Not all laws are righteous, and not everything that's legal is the right thing for people. (Mexico)

The research for this project netted me a lot of frequent flyer miles, something that feels like less of a joke now that I am more aware of the environmental damage caused by air travel. Between the initial outreach and the fieldwork, I visited ten cities across seven countries and three continents, not including the United States. During this extended process of travel, observation, conversation, interviews, data analysis, and repeat with the next place/trip, some regional patterns began to emerge from my notes and interview transcripts. This chapter will try to provide some window into the social and historical contexts that shape the experiences of the activists I met and how those contexts and experiences varied across continents, using the issues that emerged here as a guide at times for some background research. In regard to Africa and Latin America, I assume many English-language readers will not have had the opportunity to travel widely in these parts of the world, so I offer brief descriptions of my personal observations of the cities I visited in hopes of bringing them to life in ways that are not based on media representations and news stories.

As with any sociopolitical issue, regional factors have shaped the development of the movement for SMA, even as similar forces are also at work across different locations. For example, global obsessions with drug prohibition and trafficking affect the discourse around abortion medication in the United States and to some extent in Latin America, but not in Africa where economics and infrastructure shape access to medications far more than the US War on Drugs.

This chapter will offer an overview of the global shape of the movement, including its regional particularities, with the goal of making the movement visible as a complicated whole. Transnational research on social movements can't provide the kind of deep background on the historical processes that shape a movement in a particular country, but interviews and observations across diverse locations reveal patterns that are less visible in a deep dive in a single location. The regionally focused sections in this chapter build on what activists shared during informal conversations and interviews, and my own observations as I traveled in different countries talking with feminists about abortion and all the different places that conversations about abortion can take us.

Abortion Law, Colonialism, and Neocolonialism

Chapter 1 offered a quick overview of the history of abortion law in the United States, and it seems useful to go into an equally brief but somewhat more global history at the start of this chapter.

Abortion laws were initially imposed in Latin America and sub-Saharan Africa in the context of European colonialism, and are currently affected by a global antiabortion movement based in and funded by the Global North. For that reason, it does not make sense to discuss abortion law separately by region, as the origins and politics reflect global power dynamics more than locally specific processes. The international nature of abortion policy and politics can be obscured at the national level but comes into focus when you step back to look at the big picture.

As in the United States, abortion in Europe and Britain was tightly restricted in the 1800s as part of the formalization and professionalization of medicine but began to open up in the 1960s and '70s.[1] Britain legalized abortion on relatively broad grounds in 1967, and London became a center for women seeking abortions from continental Europe as well as Ireland.[2] France legalized abortion in 1975, after several years of not enforcing earlier restrictions. Portugal did not broadly legalize abortion until 2007, and was the site of the first, experimental, abortion hotline, as described in chapter 1. Poland has gone in the opposite direction, as abortion was legal and quite normal under communism, but the transition to capitalism has brought increasing restriction on abortion rights and access, driven by a resurgent connection between Catholicism and the state.[3] By the mid-2010s, Polish women largely accessed abortion through travel to neighboring countries and through the use of medication and the support of SMA activists.[4] The Polish right wing continues to gain political power, and in 2021, a Polish activist was charged with providing abortion medication to a woman, the first such case in Europe.

The Republic of Ireland illustrates a common colonial and postcolonial pattern, as abortion was initially banned under a British law that was incorporated into the legal system of the new republic, and then continued long after the original law was overturned in Britain. In general, colonial powers impose their own legal system onto occupied territories and peoples, as Britain did with Ireland as well as other colonies, and this affects the laws and legal systems created after liberation and the establishment of an independent country. When Britain changed its abortion law in 1967, this had no impact on any of its former colonies where the original British law (or some variant) may have continued to be in effect. For decades, the Irish Republic banned abortion for any reason, and even passed a constitutional amendment to protect the "unborn" in 1983, although there was a long-standing and relatively open practice of abortion-related travel to Britain as well as more recent use of medication.[5] As Latin American countries declared independence from Spain and Portugal, mostly in the 1800s, they also inherited colonial-era laws—and, of course, the Catholic Church whose opposition to abortion has only grown over the past hundred years. In sub-Saharan Africa, the legal status of abortion also largely reflects the continuation of pre-independence laws originally imposed by European colonial powers in the nineteenth century, with some modifications over the past fifty years or so.[6] While some countries—including Ireland (2018), Argentina (2020), and Colombia (2022)—have fully legalized abortion, access overall remains highly restricted across both Latin America and sub-Saharan Africa, and the regulation of gender and sexuality has now become the focus of political struggles with twenty-first-century dynamics.

During the twentieth century, the majority of countries in Latin America passed laws allowing abortion under very limited medical circumstances, but there are also countries where it has been banned altogether. The relationship between history, law, and practice can be complex and nonlinear. In Chile, for example, a 1931 law permitted doctors to perform "therapeutic" abortions for health reasons, which were increasingly available until the military coup in 1973 overthrowing Allende's socialist government. The Pinochet dictatorship first functionally banned abortion and then explicitly prohibited it in the constitution written by the dictatorship. In 2017, a new law offered narrow legalization under three conditions—to save the life of the mother, in cases of grave fetal anomaly, or for pregnancies resulting from rape or incest—which brought Chile in line with much of the rest of Latin America. Three other countries that completely ban abortion for any reason also imposed those laws relatively recently: Honduras in 1985, El Salvador in 1998, and Nicaragua in 2006. In all three countries, the laws were changed under democratic governments and not military dictatorships. In 2021, the (elected) government of Honduras amended the constitution to include a ban on abortion, apparently in response to the legalization of abortion in Argentina in 2020. Clearly, these laws are not historical remnants but emerge from contemporary political struggles over power, authority, Christianity, and women's rights, as has been true in Poland and in the United States in the decades since the *Roe* decision.

Abortion in Latin America also offers interesting examples of the interaction of law and practice. Prior to 2020, Brazil and Argentina had similar laws restricting access to abortion, but activists could work openly in Argentina and were severely criminalized in Brazil. While the laws on abortion itself were similar, Brazil systematically criminalized access to medication and any assistance to or support for women in regard to abortion, which had far greater impact than the laws directly regulating abortion itself.[7] Texas followed an analogous path in September 2021 when it criminalized providing any assistance to someone seeking an abortion, with even taxi drivers potentially vulnerable to civil suits. In contrast, the widespread use of misoprostol throughout Latin America offers an example of the power of practice over law, enabling safer nonlegal abortions and lowering the maternal mortality rate.[8]

In sub-Saharan Africa, the legal status of abortion also largely reflects the continuation of pre-independence laws originally imposed by European colonial powers in the nineteenth century, with some modifications over the past fifty years or so.[9] The African Union's human rights protocol includes language on abortion, but the legal criteria for its provision are limited to preserving the life and health of the mother, cases of rape and incest, and instances of grave fetal anomaly.[10] These limited criteria for legal abortion are a common form of restriction around the world and they account for a very small number of abortions in any country; they do, however, represent reasons largely beyond a woman's control and therefore a way to allow a narrow window of controlled legality while still denying women's autonomy. The mortality rate from unsafe abortions in sub-Saharan Africa is the highest in the world, despite ongoing improvements in postabortion care, although this reflects a general lack of social, economic, and medical resources more than simply a restrictive legal environment.[11] There is a growing feminist movement for SMA in sub-Saharan Africa, but it cannot, by itself, address the larger resource limitations and development issues confronting the region, nor the global economic systems that have stripped wealth from the continent (and continue to do so).

Contemporary antiabortion organizing first emerged in the United States in the 1980s and '90s, and has spread to parts of Europe and Russia to form a politically far-right "pro-family" movement that brings together the Catholic Church, the Russian Orthodox Church, and evangelical Protestants. This movement has deliberately expanded into Latin America and parts of sub-Saharan Africa in ways that have deeply neocolonial implications, spending significant time and resources spreading deeply conservative Christian theology and associated policy initiatives.[12] These global right-wing networks affect feminist organizing for SMA in ways that will be touched on in this chapter and then further explored in chapter 4 as part of a discussion of risk and security. It's important to emphasize that while the antiabortion far right was a salient background presence in many places, it was never central to thinking about regional patterns and experiences. The next few sections will focus on the different regions where I did research before stepping back again at the end of the chapter to bring some of the pieces together.

Africa

I had been in South Africa, primarily Durban and the Cape Town area, for conferences and postconference vacations before my trip to Lagos and Nairobi to learn about self-managed abortion. For those who have not traveled in sub-Saharan Africa, each of these is a fundamentally different place culturally, economically, and geographically. Each of these cities offered a different encounter with urban Africa, although the tourist-accessible parts of Durban and Cape Town reflected a deeper and more recent history of European dominance. In Lagos, I stayed in a less expensive hotel in one of the wealthier districts, which I discovered meant that it largely served Black middle-class travelers and young White students. In Nairobi, I again chose one of the less expensive but slightly higher-rated hotels, where there were more amenities and an interesting international mix of traveling NGO staff. Lagos is a massive, sprawling city with a kind of entrepreneurial chaos that felt familiar from various places where resources are scarce but energy and motivation abundant; I don't say that to romanticize anything, since poverty was brutally visible even in high-income areas, just to recognize that chaos and entrepreneurial energy were equally present. The districts I visited in Nairobi all felt more contained, a functional city going about its business—as was its airport, in the best of ways, unlike the international airport at Lagos which I'll just recommend avoiding if at all possible.

Despite the differences in the two cities, the NGOs housing the hotlines have many similarities. One of the most striking things about both was the sophisticated technology of the hotline call centers. In contrast to the cell phones in common usage among Latin American collectives, the African hotlines had systems that operate 24/7, 365 days a year, with the ability to provide information, take messages, and handle a relatively high volume of calls. In Lagos, the NGO office was in an open and airy building with a kitchen on the first floor and offices above, located in a busy neighborhood that seemed neither poor nor rich, about halfway between the airport and the wealthier areas around Lagos Island. In Nairobi, the NGO office was significantly outside of the city in an area that the taxi driver described as "very good." In both organizations the hotline is part of a wider array of services, advocacy, and community organizing that embodies a broader framework of women's rights and reproductive/health justice. While Kenya and Nigeria are very different economically and culturally, the staff in each place described working within complex local cultural mixtures of modern, colonial, and traditional beliefs and practices around gender and sexuality, all influenced by and interacting with Christianity and Islam.

The two countries have significantly different histories in relation to HIV, which in turn shapes the realm of women's reproductive health care through the medium of US international funding for HIV. Nigeria, in West Africa, has been less affected by HIV than many other African countries, with adult seroprevalence around 1.3 percent, and the women's health and rights organization in this study emerged from work on women's rights and health broadly. In contrast, Kenya, in East Africa, has a seroprevalence rate of approximately 4 percent of all adults, and the organization in this study began with a focus on HIV that continues to be a central element of its work to this day. To put these HIV prevalence numbers in a larger perspective, the rate of HIV among adults in South Africa is 18 percent, while in Latin America it is around 0.5 percent.[13]

One of the primary global funding streams for HIV/AIDS is PEPFAR, or the President's Emergency Plan for AIDS Relief, originally created by George Bush in the early 2000s. PEPFAR funding is affected by the Mexico City Policy, also known as the "global gag rule," which requires that international health organizations receiving funds from the United States do not provide *or even talk about* abortion with their clients (hence, the "gag"). For many organizations reliant on US funding, this has largely severed connections between HIV prevention and care, on the one hand, and abortion and reproductive health services on the other hand.[14] The executive director of the Kenyan NGO described the impact of this for the development of her organization:

> One of the major decisions we had to make early on is that we were never going to take PEPFAR money, even with a democratic president, because we understood that when we take the money in a favorable term, when that changes, it leaves us vulnerable.

The gag rule was first imposed by President Reagan in the 1980s and since then has been lifted by Democratic presidents and then reimposed by Republican ones. Consequently, as a sex worker activist I spoke with in Nairobi put it, their ability to (openly) work with and even refer people to the local organization that educates women about medication abortion is determined by who is president in the United States. (She managed to say this without implying that I might have some responsibility for this situation, which seemed both fair and remarkably generous under the circumstances.) The NGO in Nigeria is less affected by these calculations, and while the NGO in Kenya that runs the abortion hotline cannot receive PEPFAR funds, they have clearly benefited from the nongovernmental global networks around HIV prevention and care in other ways, including financially.

In relation to the politics of gender and sexuality in sub-Saharan Africa, it is also important to recognize that Christian right-wing organizing has become well established through much of the continent. Networks of evangelical churches, most with ties to the United States and other powerful international right-wing groups, exist in many countries and exert increasing pressure culturally and politically.[15] The NGO executive director described the impact in Kenya:

> There is such a growing opposition in Kenya. We see it even in the laws, and policies, and the way we are making steps back on some of the things . . . The main face that we have seen is CitizenGO. There's a new outfit called the Kenya Catholic Professionals Forum. So, Pearls and Treasures, which is—what do they call—crisis pregnancy centers.

The evangelicals are generally more conservative overall than Catholics, teaching a theology compatible with highly individualistic neoliberalism, while the Catholic Church may be deeply conservative on gender and sexuality but relatively progressive on other socioeconomic issues.

In general, religion and religious opposition to abortion wove through personal stories among activists in Nigeria and Kenya more than anywhere else, as these women negotiate lives that bridge work at a feminist NGO with communities and home lives that include religious beliefs (including their own) and institutions. While the organized Christian far right occupies a central location in political and security discourse in Africa as elsewhere, Christianity and Islam were integrated into the lives of activists in an ordinary, day-to-day way independent of political organizing.

Latin America

The large cities of South America are relatively wealthy, in global terms, with commercial centers and solid middle-class residential districts that feel familiar from a Euro-American perspective. In Santiago de Chile, I stayed in very compact one-bedroom apartments in large, modern buildings where it was clear that so many units had been "Airbnb'd" that the doormen effectively ran luggage rooms, facilitated key transfers, and answered questions about the city. I visited two other Chilean cities, Valparaíso and Concepción; of the two, Concepción felt more modern and in places a little Western-generic, while Valparaíso was unique, very beautiful, and its city center had retained some of its old character as a working-class port city. The center city of Buenos Aires felt very European without the compactness of Western European cities, and somehow extraordinary, even to this well-traveled New Yorker. I experienced both Quito and Mexico City as less Europeanized than the cities of Chile and Argentina, and the Indigenous heritage of Ecuador was visible in multiple ways throughout Quito.

The history that felt most present in the South American interviews was of the US sponsored and supported military dictatorships of the 1960s–80s and the still-present legacies of resistance to them. These connections were strongest in Chile, where Pinochet's government left behind a complete ban on abortion, but were present in other ways throughout the region. Virtually all of the activists I spoke with grew up in the long shadows of the dictatorships and the memory of leftist resistance movements that opposed them, and in Chile this threaded through stories of family, politics, and young adulthood regardless of where a family stood on the political or class spectrum. Two voices from Chile:

> My parents were involved as people who stood up against the dictatorship . . . My dad was in the railway union. A union that suffered a lot of persecution . . . Anyhow, my mom had been pretty scared, having young children like that and living in constant fear of being accused of something.

> My paternal grandfather, he belonged to the right-wing Renovación Nacional [National Renovation] party, and so my whole family benefited in some way from the dictatorship . . . My father is a mechanic, he used to fix up the local cars . . . [At school] I said, "I'm going to join a political party" and my dad said, "No [don't join any party], because that's what divided the country under the dictatorship. Lots of people were persecuted for being party members, I don't want it to happen to you."

A Chilean law professor bluntly told me that Chile would continue to be locked into a postdictatorship transition until Pinochet's constitution was overturned and a new one created. In 2021, Chileans voted in a national referendum to overturn Pinochet's constitution and write a new one, but in 2022 the first version of a contemporary constitution was not approved, sending the process back to the drawing board.

The continuing salience of this history of dictatorships and resistance is not limited to Chile. From Ecuador:

> I was eight years old and I found this newspaper folder . . . It was [my father's] identity document but it wasn't in his name, there was a different name . . . It was his combatant ID, under an alias . . . In Ecuador we say we had a soft dictatorship, but in a very repressive context: my uncle was one of the leaders who was jailed and tortured . . . Some of them died, while my uncle was imprisoned for several years, and so was my dad.

In Brazil, former President Jair Bolsonaro explicitly invoked the Brazilian dictatorship as part of his claim to power and used it to threaten progressive politicians as well as grassroots activists, reflecting the continuing power of memory across the region. However, the era of dictators created legacies of resistance as well as memories of repression, and these legacies continue to shape feminist organizing throughout the region.

The following chapters on strategies (3) and networks (6) will explore in detail how activists worked together throughout Latin America in the late 2000s and 2010s, but here I want to note that these twenty-first-century networks emerged from the twentieth-century struggles and organizing of Latin American feminists. While the movement for SMA created its own informal, and at times formal, networks among activists and collectives throughout the region, the initial rapid spread of information reflected long-standing activist relationships. The Encuentro Feminista de America Latina y el Caribe (EFLAC), where members of the Ecuadorian hotline collective did a workshop in 2009, dates back to 1981; when the first EFLAC met in Bogotá, much of the region was living under dictatorships. Contemporary Latin American feminism emerged in this context of militant struggle, deep anti-colonial and anti-imperialist movements, and a growing human rights discourse that created some degree of regional identity and interconnection. The strong regional character of organizing for SMA, with its extensive reach from Mexico through the Southern Cone, reflects the ongoing reality of a distinct Latin American feminism built on dense networks of alliance and communication across borders. It is this that enabled the relatively rapid spread of new strategies for direct action around abortion.

Another way the deep history of feminist organizing in the Americas was visible within the movement for SMA came from the growing attention to gender-neutral language around pregnancy, which I have largely adopted. In 2017–19, there were active conversations and debates about what it meant to use gender-neutral language, which is not easy in Spanish, like "*personas con un embarazo no deseada*" (people with an undesired pregnancy), and a growing recognition of trans and nonbinary people within the movement as activists as well as people seeking abortions. These conversations combined the linguistic and the ideological since the movement, like many feminist movements, had strongly centered a language of solidarity among women and, at times, of creating safety through exclusively female spaces. In the United States, arguments over the inclusion of transpeople in "women's space" have generally focused on the presence of transwomen, and the boundaries of who "counts" as female. In regard to abortion, however, the trans/nonbinary question centrally involves transmen and others who do not identify as women but have the capacity to become pregnant, which also profoundly challenges essentialist models of gender but through a different pathway. A transman or nonbinary person with an unwanted pregnancy calls into question a definition of safety based on the exclusion of men, but does so from a vulnerable location that is familiar to people who identify as female. Across Latin America, collectives have moved towards openness to the full diversity of persons who can become pregnant, which has required opening up their understandings of both gender and the construction of safety.

The SMA collectives across Latin America focus on abortion specifically but base their work on a broader political analysis that disrupts the potential for "siloing" abortion off from other issues as can be seen in much of the United States. The framework of "women's rights are human rights" that emerged in response to the brutal political repression of military rule locates feminism—including abortion—within larger discourses of liberation. While SMA collectives may have a narrow focus in their work, their stance of action based in solidarity and on women's autonomy locates them within the realm of reproductive justice, not the mainstream framing of abortion as "choice." The rejection of neoliberalism has been integral to radical strands of Latin American feminism from early on, emerging as Pinochet created the first neoliberal economic system in Chile with devastating economic as well as social consequences. As a result, the North American discourse of abortion as "choice" has little resonance in Latin America, and the struggle for abortion sits firmly within larger feminist discourses around bodily autonomy and human rights.

Notable, too, is that abortion rights in Latin America have significantly expanded across the region in the last few years, starting in Argentina and then followed by Mexico and Colombia. In Chile, the complete ban on abortion established by Pinochet was modified in 2017 to allow limited access, and for much of 2022 there was the tantalizing possibility that abortion rights would be guaranteed within a new Chilean constitution. The first version of a new constitution was defeated at the polls, but attitudes toward abortion have opened up significantly in Chile over the past few years in a process of partial *despenalizacion social* or "social decriminalization." These victories reflect the success of the human rights–based frameworks of Latin American feminists—for example, Mexico's high court effectively removed abortion from the criminal code—as opposed to the narrow and privatized strategies of the more individualist approach that has been dominant in the United States and has led to the decades-long erosion of access that culminated in the *Dobbs* decision.

In Latin America, religious opposition to abortion has historically come from the Catholic Church, which has now been supplemented by evangelicals and the global "pro-family" right. These networks of far-right actors will be explored in more detail in chapter 4, but a few elements are worth mentioning here from a regional perspective. The Spanish organization Hazte Oir has extended into Latin America, building on common postcolonial linguistic and cultural connections to enact a form of anti-feminist/

anti-LGBTQ+ neocolonialism. (It is worth remembering that current systems of gender and sexuality in Latin America are a product of Spanish and Portuguese colonization and the brutal imposition of Catholicism). The evangelical churches, unlike Catholicism, bring an explicitly neoliberal family politics that link conservative gender/sexuality ideologies to a rhetoric of familial self-sufficiency, individualism, and a "pull yourself up by your bootstraps" ideology of personal responsibility. These churches also bring an element of street-level violence to abortion politics globally, as they are breeding grounds for extremists who have been known to physically attack abortion-rights advocates and threaten visible abortion activists.

Mexico's geographic and socioeconomic location next to the imperial behemoth at its northern border has enabled it to play a significant role in transnational organizing. There's a Mexican saying, "*pobre Mexico, tan lejos de Dios y tan cerca de los EUA*," (poor Mexico, so far from God and so close to the USA) that may need to be updated in the wake of the Mexican court decision decriminalizing abortion followed by the US Supreme Court decision that recriminalized it in many states. Perhaps something along the lines of "lucky United States, so close to the feminists of Mexico" (*suerte EUA, tan cerca de las feministas de Mexico*). Like in the United States pre- and post-*Roe*, abortion laws in Mexico vary from state to state with no unified federal policy, although the Mexican court decision removing abortion from the realm of criminal law throughout the country means that an abortion cannot be treated as a crime. In addition, misoprostol can be purchased in Mexico without a prescription, which makes SMA more easily accessible and less of a risk both for people seeking abortions and activists accompanying them.

The US-Mexico border has long facilitated solutions to problems related to medical care, cost, and access for people in the United States. For those with limited or no insurance, Mexico has long been a source of high-quality medical and dental care at lower cost than at home. In the early days of HIV, some experimental treatments were accessible in Mexico before the United States; in the present, new approaches to mental health treatment using psychedelics are more available in Mexico. Many drugs that require a prescription are available at lower cost—and without a prescription—in Mexico, and the border pharmacies often prominently display antidepressants, among other things. I have heard that some now display misoprostol next to the cash register. As Mexican activists accompany US women during abortions and assist with obtaining medication, this extends the transnational solidarity of SMA in Latin America across the border into North America. Cross-border feminist alliances did not begin with accompaniment, but there is an embodied solidarity to accompaniment that is notable, along with the decolonial dynamics of the south teaching and supporting the north that we see in cross-border SMA work.

The United States

The experience of abortion in the United States has long varied state by state, as well as by race and class, and these existing inequalities will be dramatically exacerbated in the years to come. As we move deeper into the post-*Roe* era, the variations in state law will shape the strategies of activists, abortion providers, and people seeking abortions, as the chessboard of law, enforcement practices, protections, and workarounds gradually solidifies. The grassroots side of abortion work has long been locally focused to best respond to particular contexts, even while the policy side has been more national and limited in imagination. In regard to SMA, some variation on a Mexican-style landscape may emerge, with a mix of NGOs and collectives spread out across states with different laws and local enforcement practices. The existing domestic telemedicine platforms will continue and more will probably be created, along with a proliferation of techniques for mailing pills in ways that enable maximum distribution without violating state-based medical licensing systems. People have been traveling for abortion care in the United States for decades, and the distances will get longer, with greater stresses on travelers and on the slim resources of abortion funds. This is an area where analogies to Europe break down, since the distance from Poland to Germany, for example, is less than the distance from parts of Texas to clinics in New Mexico.

In the forty-nine years between the *Roe* and *Dobbs* decisions, abortion was legal but increasingly isolated, both medically and politically. When African American feminists developed the framework of reproductive justice in the 1990s to center an understanding of "reproduction" that included women of color's experiences of forced sterilization and struggles to keep families together, it challenged both the individualist framework of "choice" and the isolation, or siloing, of abortion from all other aspects of people's lives. In the early 1970s, when abortion was still largely illegal, second-wave feminists understood abortion within a larger struggle for liberation that included sexuality, health, family life, economic access and rights, and social freedoms writ large. But over time, as the backlash against second-wave feminism gained steam, legal abortion became a "special issue." The separation of abortion care from general OB-GYN care reflects this stigmatized special status and helps maintain it, as do the violence of antiabortion extremists and the decision by medical schools not to include abortion within required gynecology training. As the Clinton Democrats infamously put it, abortion should be "safe, legal, and rare"—a long way from abortion as a human right or an essential form of self-determination.

Reproductive justice locates abortion within the framework of the right to not have children, the right to have children, and the right to raise the children you have in health and safety. None of these rights could ever be taken for granted by women of color and they are increasingly precarious for all women in the United States. After the Texas SB8 law in September 2021, which banned abortion after six weeks of gestation, the language of bodily autonomy and human rights once again began to take center stage in feminist discourse about abortion, and the official release of the *Dobbs* decision has amplified this, particularly in the streets. The rapid expansion of criminalization has motivated many US activists to reintegrate abortion into a framework of justice, rather than the individualistic framework of "choice" for the privileged and lack of access for everyone else. At this writing, all SMA websites in the United States center self-determination and bodily autonomy, but those oriented towards a service model still lean toward individual choice, while those with more of a solidarity perspective tend to use reproductive justice language.

The role of the far right in relation to abortion in the United States is well known, but a few elements of it are worth highlighting here. As described in chapter 1, the system of abortion clinics in the United States actually began as a feminist strategy to create a less hierarchical model for women's health services, but then became an entrenched and defensive structure of medical care in response to the extreme violence from the antiabortion far right. Some of the dominance of the discourse of "choice" probably also reflects a response to right-wing attacks, since privatized decisions (choices) made within families and in consultation with doctors present less of a challenge to conservative American ideology. On the whole, abortion advocates have responded to escalating right-wing assaults on women by moving towards the center rather than strengthening liberation-based arguments, part of a general retreat into a largely defensive posture. There are, of course, powerful exceptions to this, particularly among abortion funds and other reproductive justice organizers; but these have been the large-scale contours of the US movement over the past decades.

It is also vital to recognize the US role in the creation of the contemporary global far right, especially the emergence of an international evangelical Christian movement. The growth of conservative evangelical churches across sub-Saharan Africa and Latin America reflects the power of this movement in the United States, which provides significant financial as well as ideological resources.[16] From a regional perspective, the twenty-first-century international religious right could be considered a form of ideological neocolonialism that has accompanied the imposition of neoliberalism from the Global North onto the Global South.

Europe

In the global movement for SMA, the international telemedicine platforms based in Europe function as a kind of central hub. As described in chapter 1, the first telemedicine abortion platform, Women on Web, was created by Women on Waves. The early campaigns of Waves' "abortion boat" were in Europe itself: Ireland in 2001, Poland in 2003, and Portugal in 2004, with the first trial run of an abortion hotline coming out of the 2004 Portugal campaign. Waves has continued to conduct periodic campaigns but developed Web as a strategy to directly mail abortion medication to women anywhere with an internet connection and a mailing address. Former Web staff created Women Help Women in 2014 to combine telehealth with support for and partnership with local organizations in many countries. The international telemedicine platforms play a vital role within the movement for SMA globally as a place where hotlines, for example, can refer women who need access to medication. In this way, the platforms function as a service for individual women who contact them directly, and as a resource for local activist organizations in places where medication is not easily accessible. European organizations have also provided technical assistance within global networks: Web and

WHW offer medical training and support, for instance, and conduct digital security training in collaboration with a feminist institute based in Germany (see chapter 4).

The Waves campaigns in Poland and Portugal shaped the emergence of the transnational movement in two distinct ways. First, through the ongoing Portuguese hotline, from 2004 to 2007, which later provided some background experience for the first collectively run hotline in Ecuador in 2008. Second, those campaigns had an indirect influence by drawing together Portuguese and Polish feminists who worked for Women on Web and then went on to play central roles in the creation of Women Help Women. The different models for transnational work in Waves/Web and WHW reflect different feminist perspectives and organizational structures, but it's also worth noting that these models emerge from different locations within European power structures (including feminist ones). The Polish and Portuguese women who worked for Web in the late 2000s and early 2010s had themselves lived in countries with restricted access that were the focus of Waves campaigns and had a different perspective on the experience of "local partnership" than someone who had only known it from a Dutch standpoint. WHW has maintained ongoing relationships as a resource and ally with organizations and networks across Latin America and sub-Saharan Africa, and this has become central to thinking about the place of Europe within a transnational movement.

In my conversations with activists in Latin America and Africa, there was little or no reference to Irish or Polish frontline SMA activists or organizations, although these were the two European countries where SMA was central to abortion access during the time that I was doing fieldwork. The Irish victory for abortion access in 2018 did come in for some discussion among Latin American activists, but there seemed to be little direct connection among frontline activists in, for instance, Quito and Dublin. The relative absence of Polish activists (other than those in WHW) within transnational networks may primarily reflect geographic and linguistic barriers between Poland and regional activists in the Global South, but it creates an interesting silence that makes Europe appear only as a privileged place with resources for the movement, despite the steadily worsening situation in Poland and Hungary, and the rise of the far right in Spain and Italy. It also obscures the central role of European activists who have themselves experienced restrictive abortion laws. I don't say this to discount the tremendous privilege and socioeconomic power of the Global North, but to point out that transnational partnerships within this movement have been shaped in meaningful ways by northern activists with significant experiences of places and moments where the privileges of resources and access have been shakier.

Thinking across Regions

There are a few themes that emerge comparatively across regions. One is the contrast between NGOs and collectives, with their different strengths and weaknesses. Another is the way recent history has shaped the development of SMA regionally—in South America, sub-Saharan Africa, Europe, across all US states—and not just country by country. Finally, the power of human rights discourses cross-regionally within this movement stands in contrast to the individualized understanding of abortion as a strictly medical procedure within health care systems.

As will be discussed in chapters 3 and 6, the organizational structures of collectives versus NGOs shapes the experience of doing SMA work in ways that are consistent across regions. To begin with the obvious, NGOs transform activism into forms of paid work and can bring a wider array of resources to the communities they serve. The word "serve" matters here, since the collectives make very clear that they offer solidarity and support rather than "services," and this constitutes the core of their political approach. However, this cuts both ways: a recent internal survey done by a group of Latin American SMA collectives found that some members would be able to give more time and attention to accompaniment if they could receive some financial compensation for their work, and in chapter 7 activists talk about the stresses of managing the competing demands of paid work, activism, and family.[17] In addition, the NGOs have the financial and technological resources to reach a broader population, and situate SMA within a broader panorama of community work. The African and Mexican NGOs that I had contact with run hotlines or do accompaniment in places where misoprostol, at least, is relatively available without a prescription. In contrast, the US web-based NGOs, like Plan C and Reprocare, first emerged when abortion was legal but often inaccessible—and now find themselves adapting to a very different legal environment. One of the strengths of the collectives is that they can function in the most restrictive legal and social environments since they avoid government recognition of any kind. And while their work focuses more narrowly on abortion, they situate it within an expansive understanding of feminist solidarity and mutual aid. At the moment, Mexico appears to be the only country with both NGOs and collectives visibly offering support for SMA and often working together within the same networks, although the United States may well be headed in this direction.

Within each region, the recent history of the last forty to fifty years has affected the emergence of the movement for SMA by shaping the social and political arena for feminist activism. This may sound obvious, but understanding how regional histories manifest within a transnational movement can be important for thinking about feminism as simultaneously local and international. It would require a separate book to truly explore those issues, but a few basic elements can be seen in this study.

In Latin America, feminist resistance to the dictatorships of the 1960s–80s created regional networks, conferences, shared analysis, and an emancipatory identity that has carried forward into the twenty-first century. These formal and informal structures facilitated the rapid spread of hotlines through South America from 2008 to 2012, which laid the groundwork for the creation of accompaniment collectives. The particular histories of Latin American feminism also led to the early formation of hotlines in Chile and Argentina that defined themselves as lesbian-feminist, arising from the visible presence of lesbian and, more recently, gender-diverse feminist activists across the region. A strong discourse around gender diversity, pregnancy, and abortion has emerged among the Latin American collectives, and somewhat in the United States, but is less apparent in Europe and sub-Saharan Africa.

The history that was most apparent in looking at the development of the movement in Africa was, unsurprisingly, the HIV epidemic and the global response to it. The development of effective medications to treat HIV in the late 1990s affected the emergence of the movement for SMA. First, although this did not directly come up in interviews, the transnational battles over medication access and pharmaceutical patents were central to the creation of the Indian pharmaceutical industry that today produces the majority of generic medications—including abortion pills. India supplies a very large proportion of the medications available across sub-Saharan Africa, and without this supply it would be very difficult for SMA to have become an accessible reality. (This is true globally, as the international platforms all rely on Indian manufacturers for generic abortifacient drugs.) Second, in Africa, the HIV epidemic plays a significant role within regional organizing around sexual and reproductive health and rights overall, for it is of course one of the key issues that shapes sexual risk and sexual health. Third, and very present in discussions with both sex workers and abortion activists, the funding streams for HIV that make medication available across the continent simultaneously create a division between reproductive care and HIV care by periodically banning any mention of abortion whenever a Republican president in the United States reinstates the global gag rule. Thus, in much of Africa, the movement for SMA emerged from feminist networks that did not directly work on medical treatment of HIV—and their separation from the dominant international health funding streams has clearly prompted a level of autonomy and innovation.

In the United States and Europe, the movement for SMA has taken shape, and is taking shape, within regions where legal access to abortion is normalized and movements are marked by this legality or sometimes by its loss (as in the United States and Poland). The movement for SMA in Europe began with Waves' outward-facing strategy of using a Dutch boat to bring a space of liberal law (international waters) to places with restrictive laws, whether in Europe or beyond. Subsequently, however, European activists from those countries with restrictive laws were key players in creating the partnerships that helped shape a transnational movement.

In the United States, there was little that could reasonably be called a movement for SMA prior to COVID, although a few organizations had formed, like Reproaction and Plan C, and some US activists had close ties to transnational organizations and networks. COVID opened up awareness of SMA through the creation of telemedicine platforms within the United States as well as a growing number of US-oriented support and information websites, which accelerated with changes in the Supreme Court and the rapid destruction of the protections of *Roe* even before it was officially overturned in June 2022. Feminist activism returned to the streets with a more militant tone starting with the Texas SB8 law and continuing through the *Dobbs* decision, but the contours of a movement for SMA within the United States are still unclear as I write this book. In the summer of 2022, probably the most interesting and visible aspect of an emerging movement involved collaborations across the southern border with Mexican activists, centered around Las Libres in Guanajuato but with other connections that are less publicly visible. Historically, the HIV epidemic has had little connection to abortion organizing in the United States, although this arises from the overall lack of visibility of women with HIV, who are largely poor women of color, more than from funding restrictions, since domestic funding streams operate separately from internationally oriented ones. This began to change somewhat in 2022, as harm-reduction organizations that formed in response to HIV among drug users began to educate themselves about SMA.

A discourse of autonomy, self-determination, and human rights provides a powerful common thread across all regions, linking activists and organizations across very different social and historical contexts. This mutual recognition was apparent in discussions of transnational hotline meetings that took place in Indonesia in 2016 and 2018, where the awareness of shared experience transcended the language barriers. This emphasis stands in sharp contrast to the language of "choice" that has dominated the United States for so long and is now collapsing post-*Roe*, and even in contrast to the normalization of abortion as part of medical services within many European countries. The intentional stance of SMA as an autonomous form of action and self-determination for pregnant people who are deliberately stepping outside of and challenging the power of medical institutions makes it intrinsically difficult to "normalize" within existing mainstream discourse. Feminist solidarity makes the slogans "abortion is unstoppable" and "we are everywhere" into an embodied reality across the planet.

3

An Act of Solidarity between Women: Strategies to Share Information and Enable Safe Abortions

We were so angry, we announced that we women would ensure [access to] abortions . . . Because it's the same thing, legal or not legal, the procedure's the same. So we said, "Yes, we'll accompany you." (Guanajuato, Mexico)

From one perspective, it is not difficult to share information about how to use medication to have an abortion: the instructions easily fit on one page. There are many websites now that share step-by-step instructions for Mife and Miso and for Miso alone, instructions that someone can click through as they have an abortion using pills acquired from a telemedicine site, an online source, a friend, or a pharmacy. For some people seeking to end a pregnancy, all they need are the pills, instructions from a trusted, reliable source, and perhaps a friend to spend the day with them as they go through the process. Others experience layers of complication related to their life circumstances—maybe associated with the pregnancy itself but also maybe connected to that moment in their lives, their relationship with a partner, the difficulty of finding space to safely abort, or a sense of isolation around the entire experience. The circumstances surrounding pregnancies and the decision to end them are as various as the people making the decision, and SMA activists encounter that full range of human experience. In turn, the strategies that have become central to the movement for SMA are grounded in the realities that shape pregnancies, abortions, and lives.

There are a few core strategies for education and support that have emerged and spread around the world, adapted to local conditions. There is some fact-sheet-level basic education, but beyond that all strategies involve direct communication between a trained, experienced activist and a person thinking about ending their pregnancy, and some include or are centered on an in-person encounter. Most use technology to mediate at least the initial contact between someone seeking assistance and the activists who respond, which allows anonymity but more importantly enables communication at a distance. Cellphones and web-based communication apps mean that the hotline in Quito, Ecuador, can receive calls from women living anywhere in the country. International telehealth platforms respond to emails from all over the world, and their staff do so from equally dispersed locations. In late 2021, after the US Supreme Court heard oral arguments in the *Dobbs* case and the comments of some justices indicated a willingness to overturn *Roe*, the director of a feminist organization that does accompaniment of SMA in Guanajuato, Mexico, made a public offer to accompany women in the United States during an interview with Jorge Ramos on Univision. Given that most accompaniment of first-trimester abortions is done via text and phone, this was not merely a symbolic or rhetorical offer—and Las Libres, the NGO in Guanajuato, is now part of a network of Mexican feminists who are, in fact, accompanying women in the United States during abortions.

The overarching legal framework for the movement for SMA is the right to share and receive information—in this case, about the safe and effective use of medication for abortion based on the WHO's formal guidance and related research. Even in places with severe restrictions on abortion, people have the right to share information, and it is difficult to imagine a prosecutor successfully charging someone with sharing a WHO protocol that can be downloaded in more than a dozen languages. However, as is already clear and will be explored in more detail in the rest of this chapter, the power of this movement comes from the ways activists support pregnant people that go well beyond just sharing information in a literal or narrow fashion.

It is important to note that the legal constraints on the interactions that take place around "sharing the protocol" vary by country and seem to have changed over time as well. Brazil has systematically criminalized many forms of assistance with abortion as a deliberate attack on feminist activists.[1] In 2021, the state of Texas began to go down this path with laws that specifically criminalize any form of assistance with abortion after six weeks (SB8), such as transporting the pregnant person or making phone calls, and the prescribing or mailing of abortion pills (SB4). Other US states have similarly banned telemedicine for abortion, but unlike in Brazil (and Texas) the US laws usually target doctors more than activists—although this may change in the coming years. The behavior of prosecutors has been fairly consistent across countries and even continents: with few exceptions, the people prosecuted for SMA are generally not activists but are women from marginalized, vulnerable social groups who are reported (often by doctors or family members) for having an abortion. The only prosecution of an activist that I am aware of is happening in Poland as I write this book, and she has been charged with providing medication. In practice, the movement for SMA operates in gray areas of the law, with some aspects of the work clearly legal under the right to information and other aspects at least pressing against the boundaries of that framework.

The core strategies used worldwide are hotlines, accompaniment, web-based communication, and community work of various kinds. Most organizations do more than one of these things, and many also engage in advocacy via community organizing and/or social media. Active conversation, at least as an option, is central to all of these strategies, although it may not be with the same person or use the same medium: for example, someone might call a hotline for support two or three times but talk with a different activist each time, or talk by phone to get basic information and then exchange text messages during an abortion. It's worth noting that community work is the only strategy that is not primarily organized around and through digital technologies, and that centrally involves a direct, personal encounter, whether one-on-one or during a workshop or public event. Accompaniment often includes moments of personal encounter, but also makes extensive use of digital technology. All require the ongoing engagement of activists who have taken the time to be trained in SMA, who create space in their lives for this work, and who commit to being present with people for whom the circumstances surrounding a pregnancy and the decision to end it are complex or difficult.

Hotlines: *Aborto seguro*

Since the rise of the telephone, the hotline has been a crucial tool for social and medical emergencies, including hotlines for domestic violence, child abuse, runaways, HIV/AIDS, LGBT youth, and suicide—indeed, the phone number for a suicide hotline is still listed at the end of print-media stories about suicide, and often appears in the crawl under relevant visual media news segments. The Jane Collective in Chicago posted flyers that said "Need an abortion? Call Jane" with their phone number.[2] Telephones enable communication that can be anonymous and yet allow for deeply personal discussion of stigmatized issues. In the twenty-first-century world of cellphones, hotlines can be easy to access and relatively inexpensive to operate, and for this reason they have become central to the experience of abortion in many parts of the world. Hotlines are less easy and straightforward to run, however, and the juxtaposition of distance and intimacy embodied in a phone conversation can be challenging for those who answer a hotline phone.

As described in the last chapter, the abortion hotline had a limited, improvisatory trial run in Portugal from 2004 to 2007 before being launched in a more definitive way in 2008 in Ecuador. In both Portugal and Ecuador, the hotline was originally intended as a way to reach the Waves boat during its offshore visit, but then became autonomous when the boat campaign was unable to go ahead as planned. In Portugal, the Waves boat was trapped offshore by the Portuguese Navy, and everyone was making it up as they went along. The hotline was originally supposed to be discontinued after the boat left, but one woman kept it going for three years until Portugal fully legalized abortion:

> Initially the organizations continued the hotline . . . Then they decided they wouldn't continue . . . I decided to do it myself . . . and I got support from Women on Waves in the sense that they sometimes gave money to pay the mobile phone bill, and I could contact them when I had questions.

Despite the obvious challenges for the young woman taking sole responsibility even for much of the financial costs, she began the story by saying, "That's why we did it in Ecuador, because we had a good experience [in Portugal]." In 2008, she was on the staff of Waves/Web, and was part of the team that went to Ecuador.

As described in chapter 1, everyone involved in the Ecuador campaign knew in advance that the Waves boat had been in an accident and still decided to go ahead with the hotline anyway. In 2008, the hotline was joyfully and provocatively launched with a banner dropped from a prominent statue of the Virgin Mary in Quito, the capital city of Ecuador, displaying the phone number.

The banner also launched a phrase that would become ubiquitous throughout Latin America, appearing in graffiti, flyers, and stenciled street art, along with a local phone number: "*Aborto Seguro*," safe abortion.

A single, committed person can maintain a phone line, but initiating a regional strategy that becomes a movement requires a well-networked collective. The decision to launch Salud Mujeres can be told as a key moment in the birth of a movement, but it also reflected the surrounding political energy of the country. In 2008, Ecuador was in a period of significant transformation: there was a new president, Rafael Correa, and a Constituent Assembly had recently been elected to write a new constitution. Progressive social movements were very active and worked closely with each other, helping to drive the political and social changes that were taking place through all levels of society. It was in this moment of overall social mobilization that a feminist-led youth NGO decided to launch the first ongoing, autonomous abortion hotline. As one of the hotline founders described it,

> The NGO had worked in [human] rights and sexual and reproductive health. But, also in youth political participation . . . We had done a lot of alliance work. So, we felt very supported . . . Many of us had links with other movements and other organizations. Also, since Correa had just won, many of us had links with people who were now in the government.

The Ecuadorian activists were part of regional feminist networks as well, and word of the hotline spread rapidly. A Chilean woman who was part of a feminist organization in Concepción said her organization received an email with a video of the launch in Quito, and they were very excited by it; long-term members of the group in Concepción reached out to women they knew in Ecuador to learn more, and work began on setting up a hotline in Chile. In

2009, the Ecuadorian collective did a workshop on abortion hotlines at the Ecuentro Feminista de Latinoamerica y del Caribe (EFLAC), and knowledge of the new strategy spread rapidly through feminist networks. New hotlines were established in Argentina, Chile, and Peru by 2011, and continued to spread through Latin America, the Caribbean, and subsequently much of the world. Once the initial team in a country had been trained, they could train subsequent members and new collectives as knowledge about abortion, medication, and hotlines was shared and adapted within and across feminist networks. For example, in Chile and Argentina, activists were trained in medication abortion and running a hotline by a member of the Ecuadorian collective in partnership with Waves/Web, but then the Peruvians were trained by activists from both Ecuador and Chile.

An abortion hotline could be described as straightforward to set up, but fairly complex to operate. A new hotline collective had to master medical protocols and legal frameworks, with their local variations, in addition to the day-to-day details of the phone line, such as hours of operation, how to share the phone, and, most important, how to respond to and manage callers. This required time and attention: one of the founders of a Chilean hotline described an extended, monthslong process of locating the medical protocols for medication abortion online and studying them, in addition to the formal training from Waves/Web and Salud Mujeres. And then there was the challenge of publicizing the hotline number, especially at a time when access to the internet was less universal; activists posted flyers, wheat-pasted, spray-painted, and stenciled "*aborto seguro*" with a telephone number all over cities and smaller towns. In both Ecuador and Chile, hotlines were initially conceived within existing feminist organizations and then run by autonomous collectives that split off to manage legal concerns and to focus on the hotline itself (which could overwhelm all other priorities in a small organization).

In much of Latin America, hotlines and other forms of SMA support are run by autonomous collectives, but in other parts of the world, such as Africa, hotlines are more likely to be run by feminist NGOs as part of a larger array of services. In Kenya, for example, one helpline is housed in an NGO that offers health education and related community organizing in low-income urban and nonurban communities, and was initially formed in response to HIV. This same NGO now coordinates the MAMA Network (Mobilizing Activists for Medical Abortion), with ten reproductive health helplines across sub-Saharan Africa. In Nigeria, the organization that runs the helpline emerged out of more general work organizing and educating women about their rights—including reproductive rights—with a focus on supporting women in crisis. Reproductive health and rights were central issues from the founding of the Nigerian NGO, but have become more so with the development of the helpline. In both Kenya and Nigeria, the helplines explicitly address sexual and reproductive health in general, although abortion is a central focus, and are nested within organizations that bridge service and community organizing around sexual and reproductive health and rights (SRHR in global acronym-speak).

The different language of "hotline" and "helpline" is partly a matter of translation (in Spanish it's just *la linea* or *linea aborto seguro*, meaning "the phone/line" or "safe abortion line") but is a question of focus and resources as well. The helplines of African NGOs have paid staff, are open for many more hours per week, and provide advice and counseling around a wider array of sexual and reproductive issues than the Latin American abortion lines. However, this is not universally the case: in Mexico, where support for SMA has been incorporated into two NGOs that I know of, one is primarily abortion-focused while the other is more similar to the African NGOs, in that abortion is part of a larger portfolio of work on women's rights. While legal recognition as an

NGO enables the resources that support a broad array of services, it also creates a certain vulnerability and for that reason I do not name most of the formal organizations that participated in this project.

The medical aspects of SMA are consistent no matter where you are, but the same cannot be said for the law, or for legal interpretations of what it means to "share information." As noted earlier, the global movement operates based on a universal right to information (including the right to share it), particularly information that can be found in multiple languages on the websites of highly respected institutions such as the World Health Organization. The challenge for hotline activists is that, in more punitive legal contexts, certain approaches to "sharing information" might lead one to "fall into a crime," in the words of a member of the Ecuadorian hotline. The boundaries can appear quite arbitrary: for example, when it was initially founded, the Ecuadorian hotline could return calls if someone left a message, while in Chile a returned phone call was interpreted as crossing the line into counseling or giving advice, both potential crimes. (Prior to late 2017, abortion was completely banned in Chile, for any reason including to save the life of the mother, which no doubt shaped legal perspectives and enforcement.) While it is difficult to get precise statistics, the knowledge of activists interviewed in this study combined with media reports indicate that the policing of suspected cases of self-managed abortion is much stronger in countries with absolute bans on abortion than in countries with limited availability. It is important to emphasize that prosecutors throughout the world target individual women suspected of SMA much more than hotlines or other forms of support.

The legal limits on communication concern information about abortion itself, but the restrictions on counseling, for example, don't apply to conversations about other aspects of a person's life when they call an SMA hotline. Unwanted pregnancies come in as many different forms as any other aspect of life, and many of those who call an abortion hotline want to talk about their lives and the circumstances surrounding the pregnancy—not just about how to use pills. The level of stigma surrounding abortion in many societies means that the hotline may be the only place for an open, nonjudgmental conversation. Activists from Mexico and Ecuador described their own process of learning the nuances of communication and the depth of connection that is possible by phone:

> You learn to listen and pay attention to changes in the tone of voice, to people's silences and pauses. I think the work we do on the phone is really valuable as well, because ultimately it means creating an atmosphere of trust between you and someone you can't see. (Mexico)

Calls from women experiencing different forms of violence are a not uncommon aspect of the experience of working a hotline, and learning to acknowledge the stress for activists from these calls and to provide mutual support for each other becomes part of sustaining the hotline over time.

> Women call you up and tell you their stories and often it's so heartbreaking, it's like she's telling me about being violently abused, that she was raped, and this, and that. (Ecuador)

Hotline callers bring a range of assumptions and experiences with them to the abortion hotline in ways that can render the experience more complicated for all involved. At the most basic level, there is the process of helping someone feel comfortable and gradually gaining their trust:

> Oftentimes they only call us after they've done the rounds of loads of places that refused to help them, and we can sense that, you know? Like they're on the defensive, unwilling to give away so much

> information, because they don't trust us. And then by the end of the call, it's completely different, you know? Their voice sounds more relaxed, they're even making jokes and laughing. (Mexico)

More fundamental is the question of how long the caller has been pregnant, which can hold very different meanings for the person calling and the person answering the hotline. A caller, for example, may fear being denied help if she is too far along, a common experience in places where abortion is legal. From the perspective of hotline staff, however, this is a more technical question since the medication protocol changes for different gestational periods.

> Sometimes the callers don't tell you the truth because they are scared . . . [One woman] told me her pregnancy was at five weeks. And I asked her if she was sure, she said, yes, she was sure . . . The pains became so bad, like she was shouting. She was calling me every ten minutes like, "I want to die" . . . I said, "Madam, I can only help you if you help me. Tell me the truth. How long is this pregnancy?" . . . She said, "It's four months" . . . I said, "Okay, fine. Now that I know, no problem. Don't worry" . . . And at the end of the day, it worked. (Nigeria)

Although the majority of abortions take place in the first trimester, the management of second- trimester abortions (after three months' gestation) have become a complex issue for SMA activists—as they were for the Jane Collective fifty years ago.[3] Second-trimester abortions often involve complicated social situations and more marginalized people or pregnancies, and are a fraught issue across abortion policy and care in much of the world (especially in the United States where the issue has been used strategically by the antiabortion movement).[4] During the time I was conducting field research, from 2017 to 2019, second-trimester abortions were integrated into the movement for SMA although not all collectives or collective members would help with them, largely because of the time commitment and stress involved for activists. Second-trimester abortions take longer, are more painful, and generally involve identifiable "fetal remains," not just the blood clots of the first trimester. These challenges also make second-trimester abortions more visible to others, perhaps especially medical professionals, which increases the legal vulnerabilities; a lawyer who works on SMA told me that since 2000, all US prosecutions for SMA in the United States that she knows of involved pregnancies of seventeen weeks or more.

Second-trimester SMA has repeatedly proven to be safe and effective when supported by knowledgeable activists, and has become an integral aspect of the work of the movement.[5] In reality, activists may know more about second-trimester medication abortion than many medical providers, and data presented at a conference in 2022 indicated that South American collectives may be more successful at completing second-trimester medication abortions than medical clinics.[6] However, as noted above, these abortions are more difficult, demand more of the activists supporting them, and require a more direct encounter with a fetus that is no longer an embryo. An abortion at ten weeks' gestation involves cells that are functionally indistinguishable from blood, but this is no longer true at twenty weeks. Some activists are willing to take on the emotional and time commitments of second-trimester abortions and some are not, or are not able to given the complexity of their lives. Given the challenges of these abortions, the majority of them are supported by accompaniment collectives (see next section) or Women Help Women, but some are done through hotlines as with the earlier quote from Nigeria (p. 72).

In some ways the experience of answering a hotline is similar no matter where you are, but the structure of working for an NGO creates boundaries that don't exist in the lives of members of collectives. NGO hotlines/helplines are run out of an office, with telephones and cubicles that are similar to any other call center (unless you overhear the conversations). Hotline collectives have cellphones that get passed around among collective members who answer the phone when it rings during posted hours of operation, no matter where they are. A Chilean activist told a long and funny story about a time when the phone rang while she was on the bus, and she watched the faces of other passengers—shocked, curious, trying to pretend they weren't listening—as she had an open, unapologetic conversation about abortion in a place where it is generally treated as unspeakable. Having activist work integrated into daily life instead of confined to a call center's office space and work hours can create difficult situations—as for this Ecuadorian activist when she was living with her mother, who did not (yet) approve of abortion:

> I remember the early calls, for instance, I'd lock myself into my bedroom . . . The stigma was much greater than it is today. I was living with my mom, and she was like, "What are you doing?"

In contrast, the structure of an office and a job enables someone to maintain boundaries in their personal life while sharing SMA information. As a hotline worker in Lagos put it,

> [Neighbors] don't know that I'm in the hotline, they know I work with an organization . . . When I'm working the hotline, I receive calls and then give information.

Hotlines are built from a core of feminist solidarity that draws activists into the work and provides a basis for developing trust with callers. However, for both callers and responders alike, there is an intrinsic anonymity to a phone call, no matter how intimate the conversation may become. For some, that can have a protective quality, while for others it can feel both limiting and like a reinforcement of social stigma. To address this, in the 2010s, accompaniment collectives were created in multiple South American countries to provide greater support through the abortion process and to offer spaces where people with unwanted pregnancies could learn and talk about abortion together. Two women who worked with the hotline in Ecuador and later were part of founding an accompaniment group described the origins of this shift in strategy:

> Giving information through the hotline is important, but it's just information, and we wanted and needed to go a little further. I started arguing for a physical space of presence . . . It was the first expression of the face-to-face encounter that is the spirit of accompaniment—to cut the clandestinity, to seize the spaces for ourselves, to speak aloud, was like getting rid of shame.

Accompaniment: The Practice of Solidarity

The heart of accompaniment lies in a commitment to be with someone, to accompany them, through an abortion (or other experience) and to be available for some period of time afterwards for support. In Latin America, the practice is also integral to work against domestic violence and *feminicidio* (femicide, or the misogynist murder of women), and it has also been used as a nonviolent strategy for protecting human rights defenders in various parts of the world. Accompaniment as a strategy and practice embodies solidarity: one person, or sometimes a group, makes a commitment to be present with one or more other people through an experience, to support them and, at least with human rights defenders, to literally put the accompanier's own body at risk to protect another. It is a practice of witness and physical and emotional presence. Abortion accompaniment does not generally involve physical risk—although abortions in a situation of domestic violence can be unpredictable—but may involve emotional stresses and some potential for legal risk. Activists in South America describe accompaniment as "*una estrategia presencial*," which translates literally as "an in-person strategy" but communicates being present with someone in a more holistic way.

The practice of accompaniment during abortion began in Mexico in the early 2000s, and about ten years later began to spread throughout South America. The first organized abortion accompaniment was in Guanajuato, where a women's rights organization went beyond advocacy into direct action to support women with medication abortion, as described briefly in chapter 1. Informal accompaniment is, of course, harder to document; a woman in Cuernavaca described attending a training on medication abortion given by an American organization around 2004 and starting to informally accompany women where she lived, two to three years before abortion was legalized in Mexico City. The largest accompaniment network at the time of writing is in Argentina, where the website of the Socorristas en Red lists sixty-four different collectives across six major regions of the country. Smaller networks exist throughout the region, and the boundary between hotlines and accompaniment has become less distinct over time, as the practice of ongoing support through the abortion process takes place through phone, email, and in person. One of the challenges of writing about a movement that is rapidly developing is how quickly some aspects can change even while core elements continue—but the rapid expansion and evolution of strategies signifies a vibrant movement.

Accompaniment collectives were often formed by activists who were already experienced with SMA through hotlines, allowing activists to build on existing feminist networks. This was especially true as a new collective gradually expanded through two or three waves of bringing in new members. For example, one activist in Ecuador in the group Las Comadres (the godmothers or midwives) recalled,

> We opened "Las Comadres" to a second layer, consisting of new people we could trust, compañeras we knew about—we needed more hands. So then, around December, a group of six more comadres came together.

The third expansion of the group reached beyond these inner circles when Las Comadres announced a "school" for women interested in accompanying abortions. The same activist described this process:

> We started a school, broad-based, and five hundred people applied. That was a crazy number, so of that lot we only took one hundred, and of those, eighty [showed up] . . . We needed many more hands, but we were rather mistrustful. It was all a process of letting go, letting go . . . I feel like we're still not done with the whole incorporation process, and it's been two years . . . We held classes to train people technically and medically and so on. Another thing was political education, another workshop was on relationships.

The work of accompaniment requires trust among accompaniers so that they can, in turn, build trust with women seeking abortions. It's more difficult to bring new activists into close confidence than it is to bring in activists with previous experience who are already part of feminist networks—but at a certain point, the circle has to expand because there are not enough experienced activists and "we needed many more hands." This same process of starting a "school for abortionists" has taken place in Chile as well as Ecuador, and makes it possible to bring in a wide range of new people at first and gradually narrow them down into a trusted set of new accompanists. Sometimes experienced activists join in one of these later waves as well; one of the Chileans I interviewed had been involved in the hotlines, then went to a master's program in another country, and later joined the accompaniment group sometime after returning to Chile.

As the brief and partial list of issues covered in these schools shows, technical knowledge of medication abortion is only one aspect of what an accompanier needs to know, and combining medical knowledge with political analysis and attention to relationship dynamics is crucial. An Argentinian activist described this connection among the political and relational by saying, "We make a lot of efforts to develop what I call a pedagogy of listening." This emphasis on listening as a key element of accompaniment shifts, and in some ways sidelines, the role of sharing information within the process and brings forward the interpersonal. Where answering a hotline is about sharing vital information with callers so they know how to safely use medication, the shift to accompaniment centers relationships and a more holistic support based in feminist solidarity.

The practice of accompaniment generally begins with a telephone call or an email to a widely publicized number or email address, and after some preliminary conversation moves into a combination of education and relationship-building. Whenever possible, accompaniment collectives will hold workshops on abortion that may include up to ten women who are seeking information and support, an in-person practice central to destigmatizing abortion and building relationships among women in a similar situation, as well as between activists and those seeking abortions. The groups try to build knowledge and solidarity horizontally to empower participants, and at times women in the same workshop may end up accompanying each other through the abortion process, with or without additional activist support. Accompaniment can take place by phone, text message, or in person, depending on the situation of the person having an abortion and on the resources of the collective, and electronic accompaniment meant that collectives could continue their work during COVID lockdowns.

The experience of accompaniment can be profound. In a published interview, a Chilean accompaniment activist said she thought all feminists should accompany an abortion as part of their political training, precisely because of the level of engagement it requires with the lives of women whom many feminists might not otherwise encounter.[7] An Ecuadorian activist described the work in implicit contrast to her earlier experience with the hotline:

> [In an accompaniment] you're right there with the women the whole time, so what's going on is much clearer and it's like, I dunno, I do feel it's a step forward. I mean, nothing wrong with information, but this is more than information. This is being with them. Enabling people to be there who aren't professional care workers, tell me what you want and what you need and I'll be there, we're going to weave that network.

At times this includes an awareness of significant stresses, including violence, in the life of the person being accompanied:

> You know she's living with violence—she won't always say so, but her situation is so extreme that you think, what's going on here? Sometimes she can't talk, I call her up and she says "Not now, but in an hour," then you realize something's up and maybe you can give a little bit more. You can say, "What else do you need? D'you want the phone number of a lawyer? D'you want to file a complaint?" And she can decide for herself what to do.

The commitment to a more holistic engagement with the circumstances surrounding an abortion has led accompaniment collectives to build networks of support and connection with allied professionals, as can be seen in the quote above. An Ecuadorian activist extended the framework of "accompaniment" to include the ways a network of professionals support the work of the collective:

> The network is not just made up of the people [who do accompaniments], it ends up including the psychologists, the midwives, the woman doctors and the rest, who may not be part of the collective as such but are involved in that whole protective environment that goes with the activation of the network.

While not included in this list, lawyers are central to the networks around SMA in general as key elements of support and protection for both activists and persons who abort, and, of course, some lawyers (and doctors, midwives, etc.) answer hotlines and/or do accompaniments as well as being available in their professional capacities. The level of support offered to women simply because they have an unwanted pregnancy goes beyond what many people can imagine as a political/volunteer project, as could be heard in the side comment above, "without being professional care workers." Activists address this directly, as with this woman in Chile:

> It's a different political proposition here, we're not a service. This point gets repeated in all the workshops we hold, this is not a service, we are not a company . . . It's more to do with solidarity, solidarity between women.

The intimate experience of being with someone while they self-manage an abortion may be emotionally and relationally similar across locations, but the surrounding social environment shapes the experience of collectives in significant ways. In Ecuador, for example, it is much easier to hold workshops and accompany women in the capital of Quito than in a small city like Esmeraldas, where

> group accompaniments aren't available, not yet. It's done one-to-one, that is, a woman and a Comadre, for reasons of greater security

> and privacy, plus over there the hotline number isn't that widely diffused yet.

These contextual factors are particularly important in regard to relationships with professional systems of support and care. Collectives form direct connections with the medical system whenever possible so that women who need (or want) medical follow-up can receive care that is respectful and professional, but this is much easier in large cities than in smaller cities and towns. In Argentina, for example,

> we work hard to establish friendly links with the health care system. We don't want women going anywhere they might be mistreated. It's not the same in every province, or state; some states and provinces are significantly more conservative, which makes the matter of forming alliances with the health system a whole lot more difficult.

This can have significant consequences; postabortion/miscarriage care is legal everywhere, but doctors may stigmatize and even actively criminalize someone who comes in for care during or after an abortion/miscarriage. In El Salvador, for example, women are reported to the police by doctors who justify this precisely because there is no medical difference between a medication-induced miscarriage (abortion) and one that is spontaneous. For the privileged, and even for ordinary members of dominant social groups, the medical system may be understood as a location of care, respect, and basic privacy, but for vulnerable populations and those with stigmatized conditions that system is often a source of disregard, abuse, and even a pathway to criminal prosecution. Knowledge of this fact underlies some of the emphasis on what is called supported autonomy or self-care within the movement for SMA, and shapes the necessity for accompaniment in particular.[8] Criminalization feeds on stigma, isolation, and fear, while support and solidarity provide protection and empowerment.

Community Work: "We Have Conversations about Power"

While "accompaniment" in the form I have described above is largely a practice of Latin America, there are similarities in the holistic frameworks and ongoing relationship-building that SMA community workers use in other parts of the world. If many of the strategies for supporting women with SMA in Latin America have been developed specifically around the needs of people seeking abortion care, in other parts of the world SMA has been integrated into already ongoing community-based work on gender, health, and/or reproductive rights. In particular, community health workers in different parts of the world have added education and support around SMA into their ongoing work on gender, sexuality, and health. There are some regional variations in what this looks like on the ground, but the overall pattern is the addition of medication abortion to ongoing work rather than the creation of something new and/or abortion-specific.

Sub-Saharan Africa may be the region where SMA has been most integrated into ongoing community-level health work, particularly sexuality- and gender-related health work. In both Kenya and Nigeria, the NGOs that operate hotlines have long been engaged with community-level health education and support and have folded SMA into this in a variety of ways, formally and informally. In Nigeria, the organization has always done workshops on women's rights and empowerment, and gradually added material on contraception, the prevention of postpartum hemorrhage (a standard use of misoprostol), and safe abortion. Staff do presentations at different community locations, including schools and churches, and commonly use a discussion of postpartum hemorrhage (PPH) as an entry point. As one Lagos activist described,

> I started with PPH. I use PPH as my referral points, and then I ended with safe abortion points. We find out that a lot of teachers, even male teachers, were interested in safe abortion. So, they are now coming in to tell me, "Can you tell us about that pill? How do you use it? I have someone, my girlfriend, my wife."

After a program at a church, the same activist remembered,

> I also got a referral from that church meeting. Before they would call me and say, "My neighbor wants to talk to you about that drug you talked about." I spoke to like five different women after that meeting.

In Kenya, the work on abortion has emerged within a larger framework of community organizing around sexuality, health, and HIV. Here, community health workers can engage with medication abortion directly, without the emphasis on PPH as a cover, unlike their Nigerian counterparts, and present it as one important aspect of sexual and reproductive health. However, the apparent openness in Kenya is an interesting example of how activists navigate complex legal waters: it is legal to educate women about abortion, including medication abortion, but self-managed abortion is more problematic as the law permits abortion only on grounds of the health of the mother according to a doctor's decision. One Kenyan administrator offered an overview of their work:

> We have conversations about power. We have conversations about safer sex . . . There are people on the ground that we've trained on contraceptives, trained them on reproductive health issues, and most importantly, trained them on medical abortion.

A Kenyan community worker described her work with adolescents in very direct terms:

> We have a school program for girls, where we train them about sexuality, reproductive health, and life skills . . . Now, most of the girls, since they're sexually active, you can't go and tell someone, "Stop having sex." Even me, you can't tell me now to stop having sex. Sex is sweet . . . We advise them to use family planning and practice safe sex.

In addition to work with high school students, there is an "orientation"-style program for young women going to college for the first time, to create a space for conversation about shifting contexts, responsibilities, and vulnerabilities, and a more general reproductive health week with information for both men and women. Kenyan activists walk a careful line legally as they integrate information about medication abortion into their workshops and other conversations.

These forms of community organizing have an explicit ethos on demedicalization, on knowledge-sharing as a form of building power in the community. One Kenyan worker described her role in the following way:

> I'm telling women to take care of their bodies and be proud of what they have. If you have this pregnancy and you don't want it, what can you do? That's where I come in as a community leader . . . For us as facilitators, as community workers, one rule that we have—when you go to these trainings, you always tell people don't keep quiet with the information. Go and tell someone else.

In Latin America, there does not seem to be any direct SMA-related analogue to the Kenyan community workers, although hotline and accompaniment groups engage in multiple forms of community education. As discussed in the last section on accompaniment, collectives in major cities such as Quito or Buenos Aires often prefer to begin the accompaniment process with a workshop that includes several women interested in abortion; this is less work than individual education sessions, but more importantly it reduces stigma and isolation by creating shared space among women facing a similar issue, a kind of one-time consciousness-raising group. Hotlines and accompaniment collectives periodically conduct open, public "abortion schools" or other presentations that may be advertised on Facebook and through other channels. In the mid-2010s, a few hotlines created abortion manuals that combined instructions for SMA with personal stories and political essays, and each of these had a public launch event that included readings, talks, and celebration. Hotlines, in particular, did a fair amount of impersonal public education in their early days, when internet access was more limited, by distributing flyers and stenciling or wheat-pasting the hotline phone number as well as the complete basic protocol for use of the medication.

In North and South America, medication abortion has been integrated into community organizing and community-based reproductive care in ways that are not NGO or service based but draw on mutual aid groups and other kinds of community structures. In Argentina, for example, there was a powerful and widespread community-based response to the economic collapse that began in 2001, including neighborhood groups that met at least weekly in a combination of mutual-aid and political organizing. These were neighborhood-based collectives, not NGOs or community service programs. This ongoing mix of the personal and the political, the pragmatic and the visionary, eventually came to include SMA. A woman who was involved in a neighborhood collective in Buenos Aires described what happened in their group:

> A women's community was formed in these weekly encounters . . . One of the things that emerged in that space was abortion . . . Socorristas [accompaniment collectives] are not the only ones that manage abortions in Argentina. A lot of abortions get managed inside these groups, for example. We have the phone numbers of the Socorristas, but then we make the contact and we resolve those abortions in these women's spaces in communities.

The creation of hotlines and accompaniment groups, and more recently the proliferation of online resources for SMA, enable community networks and organizations of all kinds to develop internal, mutual aid accompaniment among members. While the Argentinian community groups were in some ways unique to the 2001 economic crisis, the integration of SMA into ongoing activist work is likely to be more universal. Sex worker activists in the United States, for example, are starting to share information about SMA through their networks, and the website of at least one US needle exchange now has links to reproductive health information, including SMA. This is a different, more ad hoc and horizontal approach than the formalized and more service-oriented community work of the Kenyan and Nigerian NGOs described above.

At the boundaries of the medical system, doulas are community care workers who provide support and a form of accompaniment through pregnancy and childbirth, and some offer similar support with abortion. In the United States, there are now "full-spectrum" doulas who accompany women through a full range of reproductive experiences, including but certainly not limited to abortion. Doulas do not have formal medical licensure, although they are trained in other ways, and they can become extremely knowledgeable about the physical as well as emotional and psychological aspects of pregnancy, birth—and abortion. In Mexico, an NGO that runs a hotline and does some forms of abortion accompaniment has done SMA trainings with doulas. In the United States, most full-spectrum doulas offer support to people receiving abortions through authorized medical channels, but there is a network of doulas and midwives that will assist people with at-home abortion, although they are very quiet about their work.[9] The doula model shares a general framework of accompaniment, but within a regulated and commercialized environment with certification programs and professional service providers. As discussed earlier, activists in Latin America already talk about pushing back on the perception of their work as a "service," but the tensions between solidarity-based accompaniment and professional/commercial versions will likely get stronger as medication abortion becomes less tightly regulated, in both hemispheres.

Community activists in North America are learning from the Global South about how to incorporate SMA into their work. After working on an early study about the expanded use of misoprostol for obstetrics in impoverished and rural communities in three sub-Saharan African countries, two of the senior people on this study became very involved in SMA in the United States.[10] As one explained,

> [We] were going back and forth between these three countries: Nigeria, Ghana, Ethiopia, and back to the United States . . . We just got frustrated and disgusted by the fact that you could get better access to [medication] abortion kits in Ethiopia, in the highlands of Ethiopia, than you could here in the United States.

Access has expanded significantly in the United States, especially during COVID, but much of that comes from work done by Americans who have been involved with and learned from the expansion of SMA in the Global South.

In the United States, abortion funds have come to fill a larger array of needs than their name suggests, especially post-*Dobbs* as the financial and support needs have increased, and these funds also largely work from a community-oriented, solidarity-based perspective. Abortion funds provide financial assistance with the full extent of expenses associated with getting an abortion, such as transportation and childcare as well as clinic fees, and many will also help with the planning, doing a kind of short-term case management. The National Network of Abortion Funds has information about SMA on their website, and abortion funds are part of conversations about SMA at multiple levels. In 2018, a Southern abortion fund nested within a community-based organization hosted a train-the-trainers session with a US-based member of Women Help Women. The organization that houses the abortion fund works on a range of sexual health and reproductive justice issues, and does trainings on policy and advocacy issues as part of their community organizing. They see training in SMA as a good fit with their other work, and their statewide community networks include local activists who are well situated to share information and support around SMA; some of those who attended the 2018 training have gone on to train others, including at a state-level reproductive justice convention. There are some parallels between the community education and organizing done by this abortion fund/community organization and the Nigerian NGO; both situate their work on abortion within a larger context of sexual and reproductive health and social justice, but the Nigerian group can openly run a hotline and makes little effort to be "discreet" about SMA.

The level of concern about the legal status of SMA is higher in the United States than in most other places, and this predates the *Dobbs* decision. One of the founders of Reproaction, a group that defines itself as part of the left flank of US feminism, reflected that "I think the most radical thing we did in the beginning [2015] was the first community forum . . . about self-managed abortion. It was advertised and open to the public." Like the Southern abortion fund and the African NGOs, Reproaction's educational work covers a range of gender, sexuality, and reproductive justice issues, although they are able to be more open about SMA in part because their focus is exclusively on politics and education with no service delivery. For example, in September of 2021, in response to the Texas law banning abortion after six weeks, they did a teach-in on the steps of the Supreme Court that included yelling step-by-step instructions for SMA through a bullhorn. They are the only US organization I have encountered that does open and publicly advertised workshops on SMA, but unlike workshops in Latin America and Africa, these provide no opportunity for ongoing communication and support for people who are self-managing an abortion. Since the *Dobbs* decision, access to medication abortion has expanded within the medical system and the public conversation about SMA has dramatically increased in the United States, but the majority of it is online and still offers only a few examples of the kind of interaction or ongoing communication provided by hotlines and community workers in other parts of the world.

Web-Based Strategies

Almost all activism around SMA includes an online element. To quote an activist in the Dominican Republic, "Of course, there are some things that are done in the street, and others that are done on the internet." Like most other organizations in the twenty-first century, SMA collectives and NGOs have email, websites, and Facebook pages. Some have Instagram and a few are even on TikTok. When I emailed one of the Chilean hotlines in 2016, I received a long autoreply with comprehensive instructions for SMA—but email can also be used to accompany an abortion in a more personal and interactive way. Social media is good for advocacy, raising awareness, and generally getting the word out about SMA or anything else, but too open and public for the secure, individualized communications that can be done through phones and encrypted email. Websites can, of course, provide a bridge to secure personal communication, and telehealth is the most complex of the different web-based strategies within the movement.

It may seem like a stretch to call a website an activist "strategy," but it can be a powerful one in relation to abortion. There are websites in many languages and based in many different countries that provide accurate, easy-to-follow, step-by-step instructions on how to use medication to safely have an abortion at home. Some are of the "click here to start" variety while others come fact-sheet style or offer a manual that includes personal stories and political analysis as well as easy-to-read medication protocols and contraindications. There's even a US online zine in the form of a cartoon strip that gives instructions through the medium of a story about Sam's medication abortion. One of the Chilean hotlines put up a website that has downloadable abortion manuals in Spanish, Haitian Creole (for the largest non-Spanish speaking immigrant population in Chile), and Mapudungun (for the Indigenous population). Most, possibly all, websites include links to telemedicine platforms as a primary source of trusted medication. In all of these ways, they incorporate some of the information-sharing functions of the hotlines, but do not offer the possibility of an actual conversation. A few years ago, for example, a US-based website, Plan C, posted reviews of multiple (non-telemedicine) online sources of pills, including the results of lab tests to determine the quality of the medication (most were as labeled); the information on medications has been updated as of 2023. Most websites include links to other sites that may offer additional information; many people seeking an abortion can get all the information they need from one or two websites and have no need for communication with an activist or medical provider.

Social media seems to be used in two distinct ways: for political advocacy and for sharing general information about SMA. On the advocacy front, it is used to raise awareness of issues and mobilize for action, sharing information about policies or court cases alongside calls to turn out for a demonstration or to contact elected representatives. Political education and awareness were a particular focus of posts on Twitter, at least until its purchase by Elon Musk, including cultural work to reduce stigma and normalize abortion, and the sharing of hashtags and retweeting between feminist organizations to promote networking.

On the other hand, as with websites, social media can be a medium to share information about medication abortion in general and SMA in particular, and to provide links for more secure communication with hotlines, telemedicine, and accompaniment. Both Facebook and Twitter are used to broadcast information about SMA, including explicit instructions and contraindications as well as links to additional material. For example, one of the African hotlines was very active on Twitter in early 2021, offering explicit information about contraception and abortion, as well as political analysis of a recent policy change and advocacy for education for pregnant and parenting girls, and tweeting "If you are pregnant and scared, then call me." "Miss Oprostol" is a Spanish-language Facebook page with a sense of humor, a lot of abortion-related information, and a "call now" button that links to a Mexican accompaniment collective. Organizations that work on a wider array of sexual and gender issues often create a specific Facebook page, and sometimes Twitter account, for abortion and SMA: for example, the African hotlines each have their own Facebook accounts, as does the MAMA Network of hotlines, which are separate from the main NGO accounts on Facebook and Twitter. The telemedicine providers also use both Twitter and Facebook for a mix of political education, advocacy, and abortion education; they also provide links to their online platforms. Activists are clear that social media, despite its limitations, is good for spreading the word widely and publicly, providing basic education, and offering ways to link to more secure, personal assistance.

Unlike the other strategies described in this chapter, the main abortion telemedicine platforms operate within recognized medical systems and offer slightly medicalized approaches to SMA. The basic platform design comes from Women on Web and Women Help Women and has been adapted by others. Some US-based telemedicine platforms have tried to replicate some aspects of the clinic experience for both doctors and patients by starting with a video visit, but most use the basic model developed by the international platforms. Someone chooses a language from a dropdown list, fills out a medical form on the site, answers a series of basic questions about their pregnancy and relevant aspects of their health, communicates by email with a help desk, and, unless there are medical contraindications, receives pills in the mail. They may have ongoing communication surrounding the abortion if desired and will receive a follow-up email checking in on whether the pills arrived, whether the person has done the abortion, and if so, how it went. From the user perspective, it is all designed to be fairly straightforward and uncomplicated, a self-managed abortion with some long-distance email support. For many, the primary goal may simply be to obtain authentic pills safely and at a reasonable price. (Some sites can even provide pills at no cost, for those who cannot afford to pay.)

A much more complicated structure and experience lies behind the user-friendly interface. Chapter 1 gave a quick overview of the multiple-country structure of international platforms, which are driven by the complications of prescribing and sending medication all over the world. As a Moldovan doctor who works with Women Help Women put it,

> You should understand that me and a colleague of mine, we are using our signature to prescribe all the pills. So, authorities in some countries are quite angry with us . . . though we haven't had any serious problems with this . . . I'm not breaking the law of my country,

which doesn't say anything about if I can or cannot prescribe pills to women in other countries.

The apparently simple help desk system is actually a sprawling global network across countries and time zones. The staff who respond to email live in many different parts of the world and log in to the help desk email system during their shifts to answer whatever emails come in for their language group (English, Spanish, Polish, Portuguese, etc.). Emails are sent from around the world and are typically answered by someone in a different country than the sender; payment (if any) is processed as a donation in the Netherlands; medication is prescribed out of yet another country, generally Moldova or Austria; and the pills are then shipped from India to the person who sent the original email, as long as they can receive international mail delivery. Shipping is the weakest link in the chain of events, vulnerable to postal strikes, volcano eruptions, international pandemics, overly inquisitive postal inspectors, and anything else that closes airports or otherwise disrupts international mail systems. There are countries where pills are routinely intercepted at the border by inspection systems, as in Brazil under Bolsonaro, but for the most part they get through. To some extent, the international platforms run in the interstices of the global regulatory systems, as the Moldovan doctor's quote suggests—but they work because those liminal zones are nonetheless legal, and because a small, anonymous box that contains carefully packaged pills rarely attracts attention as potential contraband.

The work of answering individual emails is at the heart of the international telemedicine platforms, but also has a certain invisibility. Similar to the NGO hotlines, working a help desk is a job that has regular hours and does not intrude on the rest of one's life, at least not more than any other demanding job. A woman who helped create one of the hotlines in South America and later worked for an international telemedicine platform compared the two: "It was different in the way we related to women. I think it's different than speaking on the phone. So, it was kind of less personal . . . I liked it a lot because it was very practical."

An email may be less personal than a phone call, but the international nature of the work brings both technical and emotional challenges. Someone who answered emails in both Polish and English noted that there are different logistical protocols for different countries, and this was particularly challenging for the English-language team, since English emails came from many different parts of the world, each of which had its own logistics. The work of the help desk is intrinsically remote, and the conversations about what it was like to be part of a global, online team foreshadowed the experiences of many professionals who were suddenly hurled into this virtual world by the COVID-19 pandemic. One of the Women Help Women staff described her experience:

> I hadn't realized that it was very lonely work . . . You're just sitting for hours in front of a computer answering emails; that's it. And coordinating—I've also done a lot of work in terms of coordination of the teams. And that's also the same; a lot of meetings with the team members and with the rest of the organization, and then a lot of time in front of the computer.

She went on to say, "We have very strong bonds towards each other. But we don't really see each other [in person]." In addition, the work itself has to balance medical precision with the complexities of counseling someone asynchronously via email:

> Normally you have all sorts of counseling or follow-up. You have women that don't e-mail at all, women that email fifty times and constantly come with very detailed questions about medical abortion . . . So, you give a lot of attention on the counseling and the wording.

While these different strategies can seem universal, given that none are unique to a single country, there are some distinct differences between the Global South and the Global North. Support for SMA in the Global North largely comes through telemedicine, through nonmedical websites that provide information but not interaction, or from relatively low-profile community workers who incorporate SMA into a larger array of reproductive health work, often in a professionalized capacity as a doula or midwife. In both Europe and the United States, women who have difficulty accessing abortion where they live also travel to the closest location with accessible services, with assistance from abortion funds in the United States and organizations like Abortion Without Borders in central Europe, which facilitates abortion travel for Polish women. Poland has the only self-described abortion hotline that I could find in Europe or North America, although there are two SMA-oriented websites in the United States that include phone numbers to talk with someone—one offers contact with supportive medical professionals and the other describes itself as a health line with information and compassionate support. However, I write this less than six months after the *Dobbs* decision and the issue of access to abortion medication has become central to the rapidly evolving situation in the United States, so I assume things will have changed by the time this book is published and in readers' hands. There has already been a shift towards demedicalization of medication abortion in the United States since *Dobbs*; for example, in the spring of 2022 the health line mentioned above said it was staffed by doulas with training in trauma management, a much more professionalized framework than the "compassionate support" of fall 2022. In the Global South, where restrictive laws have long been common, support for SMA mostly comes from activists working in demedicalized, community-based contexts such as hotlines, accompaniment, and feminist NGOs.

This chapter has framed the work of the movement for SMA as a set of strategies for action, but it is vital to understand that the structure underlying all of these forms of action is built on solidarity, connection, and shared risk. In the United States, at least outside of activist networks, the culture defines support for others as a form of volunteerism, of donating or sharing time/expertise, that draws on older models of charity—an intrinsically vertical relationship between someone who helps and someone in need. But the movement for SMA embodies a fundamentally different perspective.

Work based on solidarity rests on the knowledge that systems of oppression affect us all, and that we share both the risks and the benefits of creating a different world. The movement for SMA emerges from this understanding that bodily autonomy and self-determination are intrinsically shared, are a right for all or at risk for all. For that reason, the hotlines, accompaniment groups, and other direct-action strategies for sharing information and support are all centered around a core structure of solidarity among women and others who can get pregnant, emphasizing a "pedagogy of listening" as well as access to Mife and Miso. As an activist in Brussels said, "They don't have to join the club of the feminists to get an abortion." The movement for SMA is not about self-help groups or charity, but about working together to change the world.

4

Being an Activist Is Not Easy: Managing Security and Sharing the Risks

We'd gotten in touch with this lawyer we trusted, and she said everything would be fine. In other words, we'd done a certain amount of legal research and risk assessment. And we felt that as this was a low-profile topic, not much discussed in the public sphere, there was no reason we'd run into any . . . legal trouble. We felt quite safe. In addition, we'd done a great deal of alliance-building. We felt strongly supported. Not so much socially, but at the level of institutions. I mean we knew that if anything happened to us, a lot of organizations would mobilize. (Ecuadorian activist and cofounder of the hotline)

For movement activists, managing risk and maintaining security is always a balancing act, based not just on the letter of the law but also on political necessity, popular support, and local context. They approach questions of risk and security through perspectives that are broader than the technicalities of the law, but also not exclusively centered on the moral or political imperatives that motivate action. For the Ecuadorian activists who founded the first safe abortion hotline, consulting a lawyer was one of the steps, but their sense of security was primarily based in a set of political rather than legal calculations. On the one hand, they had deep connections to other movements that would stand in solidarity if needed; on the other, a general lack of interest in abortion at that time meant there would be no political benefit from legal charges. The activist quoted above later reaffirmed,

> When I say we felt strongly supported, I mean it was support from people in organizations . . . We hadn't done much work around security, we weren't hardly worried about our safety.

Another longtime member of the hotline went on to draw comparisons between the early years and 2019:

> The present context is a bit more restrictive. In 2009 there weren't any women prosecuted for having abortions, and now there are. And there's something else new, too—the fact that abortion is being globally discussed, becoming a hot topic in the public arena, generates a kind of insecurity . . . [In 2010] we engaged in direct action outside the public prosecutor's office, there we were, flinging [symbolic] blood at the building and there was little risk of being arrested, but nowadays we think twice before performing those kinds of actions.

The laws in Ecuador have not changed from 2009 to 2019; however, the political and societal context has changed both within the country and internationally in ways that alter calculations of security and risk for the hotline collective.

An activist in Chile described accompaniment as taking place "*en tierra gris*" (in a gray area) in relation to the law, and these ambiguous spaces allow for approaches that don't see legality as the primary factor shaping the possibilities for action. This is not unique to abortion activism, and I can offer an example from my own experience as a harm-reduction activist. From the mid-1990s through the early 2000s, I was part of an unauthorized harm reduction/syringe distribution collective in Brooklyn, NY, that worked primarily in areas with significant homeless and sex worker populations. At the time, the New York State health commissioner had declared an extended public health emergency in regard to HIV among injection drug users, which enabled the health department to offer legal protection to formally authorized syringe exchange programs that followed certain policies; needless to say, we never applied for authorization—and couldn't, because we did not adhere to restrictive state policies. The legal and authorized programs kept us well supplied with free syringes and other materials, despite the potential risks that this entailed for them. No one involved had any meaningful legal concerns, despite the fact that our actions were technically in violation of laws regarding syringe possession and drug paraphernalia, and the authorized programs that supplied us with clean syringes violated the state policies that enabled their somewhat provisional legal status. We were all in what could be generously described as a "gray area," and our safety came at least in part from our visibility, which is also true for SMA collectives in Latin America and other parts of the world.

We operated within what could be thought of as a space of consensual blindness that included an array of official actors. The police harassed drug users but were uninterested in arresting a group of White harm-reduction activists who worked in squatter camps, sex work strolls, and other spaces that were relatively invisible to outsiders. Staff in the Department of Health branch that regulated syringe exchanges clearly knew what was going on, and occasionally joked about supply chains—but had no interest in clamping down on the situation since we were reaching high-risk populations in places that were distant from the authorized exchanges. When I began working at a research institute that focused on harm reduction, the director told me very explicitly that I could no longer pick up supplies for the collective, since that put legal programs at risk, but otherwise what I did on my own time was entirely my business. In brief, our actions were relatively quiet but quite well-known, and the legal and policy violations (by multiple parties) were systematically ignored despite being visible and tacitly recognized. Our actions and those of our allies were strategic and calculated, but formal law and policy were not the primary factors shaping the space within which we operated. The existence of legal syringe exchange programs created space for our publicly visible, unauthorized version; in places where needle exchange is completely illegal, underground programs operate more carefully but they do exist and also work within a form of negotiated "invisibility."

As with my experience of unauthorized needle exchange, SMA organizations and activists negotiate dynamics of risk that are driven by social and political context at least as much as by formal law. The Ecuadorian activists quoted above described a shift from their initial casual confidence to more careful risk management in response to changes in the larger political landscape, including an increase in the politicization of abortion and a decrease in the overall level of mobilization among allied progressive movements. An activist from Venezuela said that the socialist-identified government of Hugo Chávez wouldn't take action against them, while at the same time noting that her experience was in Caracas, and that the experience of compañeras in the smaller cities was quite different. SMA organizations operate under the formal legality of the right to share information, but the boundaries of both "sharing" and "information" might be described in sociology jargon as negotiated constructions, in which the meaning of the terms and the actions they describe are not fixed or universal but emerge from the interaction of sociopolitical processes: activists assert the legality of their work while simultaneously locating it within a shifting array of threats and concerns. This is a very different way of thinking about risk and security—and even legality—than what is reflected in a direct question like, "But is it legal?"

The framework of "security" is much larger than questions of technical legality, and reflects the language used within the movement to talk about safety and risk. Abortion activists are part of larger discussions of "holistic security," a concept developed for defenders of human rights. In the movement for SMA, "holistic security" encompasses a broad array of issues for both activists and the people they work with, ranging from digital security to social and emotional stress to managing threats from right-wing evangelicals and the police. I want to emphasize that the legal concerns expressed by activists were primarily about the risks for people having an abortion and about general police harassment of activists—not about the legal status of hotlines or accompaniment. A Portuguese woman living in Brazil referenced the change in her understanding of risk after doing this work in South America:

> I was coming from a very comfortable context—in Portugal, you just don't think about people who will threaten you because you're an activist. That does not exist.

A European woman living in Chile compared her experience of doing similar work in two very different locations:

> I'm way more paranoid now, or I wouldn't say paranoid . . . I'm way more careful. And I really understand [the need for security] . . . It's kind of difficult to understand . . . when you're sitting in Europe . . . But then all of a sudden we're on the other side and we realize that there is a risk.

It's important to modify this general reference to Europe, however, since this sense of safety was not experienced by abortion activists in Ireland before 2018—and as I write this a Polish activist is facing charges that could bring a three-year prison sentence for assisting a woman with an abortion.

Within the movement for SMA globally, discussions of risk, safety, and holistic security are built around a set of shared concepts and understandings that were just emerging in 2017–19 when I did most of my interviews. This chapter will focus on concepts and general approaches to thinking about risk and security more than specific details or tactics; the ways activists understand and assess risk change less than the particular threats and contexts they manage or the tactics and tools they use to keep each other safe. Digital security may be an obvious issue for a movement where digital technologies underlie the majority of day-to-day work, but a person's ability to follow a technical security protocol depends on their environment as well as their training. Central to SMA activists' assessment of risk, and a key element of holistic security, is the understanding that all security, even the most technical—as in digital security—requires a base level of social, emotional, and psychological stability and self-care. A sense of caution and a feeling of connection and responsibility to others increases attention to digital security, for example, while someone who is either overwhelmed or feeling invulnerable is at risk of skipping even the most elementary online precautions such as never using the Wi-Fi in airports.

As reflected in the quotes from transplanted European activists, the primary sources of threat come largely from what might be called the political aspects of the legal systems, which means that the threats are often unpredictable, exacerbating the stress on activists. For example, police harassment of activists can take many forms and may focus on aspects of life outside the realm of political work. A feminist law professor in Chile, for example, expressed frustration to me about young radical feminists who put themselves at risk by smoking pot or being associated with anarchist collectives that engaged in property destruction. A young lawyer, possibly one of her former students, described the criminalization of activists as a deliberate police tactic, and the perception by an older generation that the resulting situations were "*casos sucio*s" (dirty cases) because they involved criminal law rather than "clean" human rights issues. The law professor works from a straightforward feminist human rights perspective, while the younger lawyer has added the study of criminal law to her activist legal portfolio in response to the expansion of criminalization as a mechanism for political repression—a generational shift that can be seen in North as well as South America. The politicization of abortion by evangelical churches, for example, has increased the criminalization of abortion in many parts of the world in part by increasing the incentives for prosecutors to file charges against women for abortion—or, as in Poland in 2022, against an activist for providing medication. The younger generation knows they need to fight in the criminal courts, not just on straightforward human rights terrain.

Perhaps the most important element of thinking about risk and security lies in understanding the profound interdependence both within activist networks and between activists and women seeking abortions. There must be a minimum level of trust and confidence among everyone involved in order to balance safety and risk. An unsecured chat record on a phone could reveal a dozen identities, or more, in the hands of border security or an angry boyfriend. The case against the Polish activist appears to have been started by the male partner of the woman to whom she is accused of sending pills. A security trainer within one of the organizations describes the dynamic:

> If there's one person in the group that does not run her operation securely, we are all exposed . . . I often compare it to a commune that has open relationships. Everyone can have sex with one another within the group—that was the agreement—but if one of us goes out and has unprotected sex, and comes back to the group, we are all exposed.

Sharing Information and Shipping Pills

Much of the work on understanding the legal and law enforcement–related risks surrounding SMA for both activists and pregnant women has been done by lawyers who work in feminist and human rights legal institutions. There is an interconnected network of lawyers concerned with SMA that extends from Canada through the Southern Cone of Latin America. The legal framework for the entire movement for SMA is the right to information: specifically, to share and receive information about medication abortion (or anything else) regardless of the legal status of actually having an abortion. Activists in much of the world assume the legality of sharing information, although they recognize local variations in how this is interpreted; but there has been considerable anxiety as to whether this right applies to the United States as well. In fact, several US-based organizations have been quite openly sharing information about how to use abortion pills for several years without any negative legal consequences. As mentioned in the last chapter, Reproaction has done public, in-person workshops and even a live (and livestreamed) teach-in on medication abortion in front of the Supreme Court in September 2021. However, the anxiety accurately reflects the depth of politicization of abortion in the United States, and right-wing aspirations to control information about sexuality, health, and rights in general. It is not yet clear how the post-*Dobbs* legal terrain will evolve on any number of issues related to activism and SMA.

In practice, the right to information provides an umbrella of legality over all the forms of action described in the last chapter, although the definition of "information sharing" varies by country and sometimes even by state, region, or county. The local understanding of what could safely be said or done varied significantly between Quito and Santiago de Chile, at least in 2018, but also between Quito and the smaller, more conservative Ecuadorian cities of Cuenca or Esmeraldas. In Africa, I heard less concern from activists over what constituted "sharing information" over the hotline, but these hotlines explicitly locate abortion within a broader array of sexual information and reproductive concerns, which makes the emphasis on abortion itself less visible.

Laws about abortion itself are not the only legal issues that shape the environment of risk and threat for activists. In 2017, abortion was completely banned under any circumstances in Chile, the Dominican Republic, El Salvador, Honduras, and Nicaragua—yet the level of threat for both activists and women seeking abortions was clearly not the same across these countries. The situation in Central America was sufficiently high-risk that I did not go there for research (nor were introductions to activists there offered to me, for fear of putting the activists at further risk), and while I heard more concern in Chile than from the DR, in practice, the movement in Chile was well-established, quite visible, and rapidly expanding. In Kenya, sex worker activists primarily navigated nonlegal policy constraints that shape their access to US international HIV funds; their ability to (openly) discuss abortion with their constituents was shaped by the cycles of the global gag rule, imposed by Republican presidents and lifted by Democratic ones, but funding constraints are not the same thing as criminal law. Among the people I spoke with, only the women in Brazil expressed significant, ongoing concerns about government repression and a general (sometimes overwhelming) lack of security, which they connected to the overall political situation for progressives in Brazil under Bolsonaro, even pre-COVID. Brazil and Argentina had very similar abortion laws (prior to the legalization of abortion in Argentina in 2020), but Brazil severely criminalized access to medication while Argentina did not; consequently, the movement for SMA flourished in Argentina but has been forced underground in Brazil.[1] In purely legal terms, any assistance with medication access is the primary source of legal vulnerability for all activists other than the telemedicine platforms.

Access to medication is central to the practice of SMA, as is the ability to move medication within and across borders, but these are also the most significant points of risk for activists. Miso was available in pharmacies in many Latin American countries until it became widely known as an abortifacient and governments began to restrict access. The availability of pharmaceuticals in Africa is highly variable, although I also heard about specific issues related to Miso due to its known "off-label" uses. Hotlines and accompaniment collectives refer women to the international telemedicine platforms as a reliable source of medication, as the platforms ship Mife-Miso packets from a generic drug manufacturer in India. The packets have become recognizable to customs agents in countries that try to block international provision of abortion medication, and are vulnerable to being seized at points where international packages are scrutinized. Sometimes, medication may be shipped in bulk into a country, since it is less identifiable that way, and activists within the country then create individual packages to send through domestic mail. The women who have been involved in this in-country shipping describe it as extremely stressful, since they are vulnerable to drug-related charges if caught, and this work typically takes place within an environment of elevated repression and surveillance. A woman who had done this described the experience:

> I used to do the—I don't know, what should I call it? The—well, shipments? When I was doing those, I felt like, "Yeah, that's dangerous," because I have everything in my hands, and in the house, so it was a risky thing. But now, I'm not doing those, so I feel relatively safe.

While the movement of pills was not a focus of my research, I did learn that abortion pills cross borders in a variety of ways other than direct shipment from India, perhaps the most common of which is inside ordinary luggage. A Chilean social scientist and activist whose work took her back and forth between Buenos Aires and Santiago would periodically bring pills from the relatively open-access world of Buenos Aires to the then relatively closed environment of Santiago. A European activist had pills delivered to her mother-in-law at one point, for later retrieval, and her husband had also assisted with moving "product" around at various times. The small number of relatively high-profile SMA activists can't do this under any circumstances because, as one of them said, "no one would believe it was for my dog." The COVID pandemic threw a relatively stable system of medication distribution into chaos after the Indian airports closed down, temporarily shutting off the supply of virtually all generic medication to the Global South, at a moment when everyone was avoiding in-person medical care. Ad hoc systems of medication distribution and telemedicine emerged, largely within countries rather than across borders, at times with local doctors taking on new levels of responsibility. For example, in the United States, a team of experienced activists with extensive connections among doctors and pharmacies worked with the abortion telemedicine platform Aid Access to create a system whereby prescriptions from the platform were filled and shipped domestically, often within the state where the woman lived.

As with other pharmaceuticals that have illegal uses, there is a black market supply of Mife and Miso in medication-abortion combination packs, as well as Miso sold separately. While underground drug markets tend to have a bad reputation for the quality of their products, when the US organization Plan C ordered pills from twenty-two online sources that did not require a prescription and then lab-tested the pills for purity, they found that all pills were as labeled and close enough to advertised strength to cause an abortion; the Mife in particular was very close to the labeled strength, while the Miso was more variable.[2] Their conclusion was that the internet was a viable source of abortion pills for women who did not have other alternatives.

In addition to online sources, I spoke with two people who sell abortion medication: Mife-Miso combination packs when they can get them and otherwise Miso alone. Neither was a professional drug dealer. In 2017, a gynecologist in Santiago, Chile, gave me the email address of the man she recommends to patients who need abortions, and we met in a tea shop near the Bellas Artes metro station. He told me that he obtained medication through a variety of sources, in particular during trips to neighboring countries where it was available in pharmacies, and sold it at not much over cost to women who came to him through trusted sources. He described himself as trying to be an "ethical dealer" by selling only product he was confident about and at reasonable prices, since he had a middle-class job that provided for his needs. Unlike the activists, he was relatively isolated—he kept this work largely a secret from most people who knew him—and he didn't say much about how he came to be involved in selling abortion pills. I also spoke with a female health and HIV-prevention outreach worker in Kenya who often sold Miso to women she knew or encountered in her work. She was part of an agency that did not do abortion-related outreach but did have a lot of contact with women who needed this assistance; like the "ethical dealer" in Santiago, she saw her off-hours activities as providing a needed resource rather than seeking significant profit.

Politicization and Criminalization

Laws and law enforcement are fundamentally political processes under the best of circumstances, but when a particular issue such as abortion or drug use gets politicized, then law enforcement can cross over into deliberate criminalization as a tool for repression. A European activist working in Chile in the late 2010s went through a risk assessment with a group of Chilean feminist "movement" lawyers, which included explicit questions about possible areas of vulnerability.

> We did extensive interviews to understand who we are, what we do, what's our level of risk in our life . . . One of the things that they focused on a lot was—Do you consume marijuana? Do you consume other drugs? Do you live with people who consume them? If so, does the dealer come home or not? . . . Do you have [abortion] pills at home?

The potential for this kind of direct criminalization may seem distant to some European activists, and was surprising to the woman who told me about it—but has a long history in the United States in relation to African Americans, in particular. The War on Drugs first emerged as part of a very deliberate strategy to criminalize protest and communities closely tied to the social movements of the 1960s, and the mass incarceration of Black and Brown people for drug-related crimes turned out to be much easier than the direct repression of dissent.[3] These examples tie directly back to the earlier discussion of *casos sucios*, and the growing relevance of criminal law for human rights lawyers in many parts of the world.

The politicization of abortion has led to significant levels of criminalization, although through the more direct pathway of increasing the political and electoral incentives for conservative administrations (and prosecutors) to push for abortion-related charges across the board. The quotes from Ecuadorian activists at the beginning of the chapter illustrate this dynamic; they talk about how changes in the political environment affected their assessment of the risks associated with direct action. A member of the Ecuadorian hotline noted that while women were not prosecuted for abortion in the early days, more recently there had been some cases, which she attributed to the increased politicization of abortion both nationally and regionally.

SMA activists within the United States expressed considerable concern about the possibility that a right-wing prosecutor could decide to file charges against someone for the potential political benefits of "cracking down" on abortion, especially in states where prosecutors are elected. This can lead to highly political but legally dubious charges: for example, in April of 2022, a Latina woman in Texas was charged with murder connected to a self-managed abortion, although the charges were quickly dropped after protests erupted and it was pointed out that Texas law explicitly states that pregnant women should not be charged, only those who help them. Prior to the fall of *Roe*, women who were prosecuted for self-managing an abortion were generally women of color, and they were charged with crimes like homicide or mishandling of human remains, not abortion per se; and while that may change as abortion itself becomes a crime in some states, the choice of more provocative charges also reflects the intersection of stigma and politicization.[4] The relationship between political calculations and abortion-related charges can also be seen in the Brazilian decision to criminalize access to abortion medications, which expands the range of charges possible for SMA and makes self-managing an abortion much harder. In El Salvador, the government has gone even further and used the possibility of SMA as a justification to criminalize miscarriage on the grounds that any miscarriage could in fact be a medication abortion—although as in the United States, the actual charge may be homicide or child abuse related. There is some fear that far-right politicians and prosecutors will try to criminalize miscarriage in the United States, at least in deeply conservative states, and the Texas case above may have been a first attempt at this even pre-*Dobbs*.

Throughout the fall of 2022, the antiabortion far right in the United States began to weave together conservative anxieties about drugs, immigration, the border, and gender/sexuality to create campaigns that criminalize SMA. Conservative media promoted fears about illegal immigrants and drug smugglers bringing medication for "chemical abortion" across the Mexican border. Some media stories rhetorically linked this to Mexican drug cartels and the violence associated with the transportation of heroin and amphetamines, while others focused more on the image of undocumented immigrants sneaking across the border with questionable pills to sell to vulnerable US citizens (implicitly represented as young White women). This deliberate strategy of using ideologies of the White nationalist far right and the entrenched racism of the War on Drugs within antiabortion organizing grows out of long-standing affinities among these strands of the US far right, but the deliberate focus on the movement of abortion pills across the Mexico border is no accident. As discussed in earlier chapters, Mexico offers access to high-quality pharmaceuticals, including abortion pills, at lower cost than in the United States, and there are powerful cross-border alliances developing among US and Mexican feminists. The antiabortion movement has begun to systematically target and criminalize cross-border support for SMA using language and potential criminal charges that center drugs and immigration, not abortion.

In the twenty-first century, the politicization of abortion has become a global dynamic rather than a matter of domestic politics within any one country. After Argentina legalized abortion through fourteen weeks, Honduras wrote a ban on abortion into their constitution. US- and European-based "pro-family" organizations have established a permanent presence at the Inter-American Court of Human Rights, and supported the El Salvadoran government when a case about a woman incarcerated for suspected abortion came before the court.[5] While the Catholic Church continues to be deeply opposed to abortion, the religious force driving anti-abortion campaigns and movements in much of the world today emerges from evangelical Protestant churches. A Brazilian activist went so far as to say that the Catholic Church wasn't an ally but also was not particularly a problem in her experience. In much of Latin America and Africa the spread of evangelical Protestant churches has brought a sometimes-violent focus on conservative gender roles and "traditional" family structures, and a demonization of abortion. In Poland, however, the cultural merger of nationalism with Catholicism has driven the increasing restrictions on and prosecution of abortion in that country.[6] The dynamics of risk, security, and global far-right antiabortion politics will be explored in more detail a little later in this chapter.

Openness, Discretion, and Social Context

Cultural change happens gradually—and unevenly—in ways that both reflect and shape the work of social movements on the left and the right, and that shape the contexts within which SMA activists work. In every country I visited, when asking about the risks of SMA work, I would hear more about the social environment than about the law. In the United States, right-wing movements have been highly visible actors on the public stage for many years, reshaping the cultural conversation as well as judicial and legislative action. In much of Latin America, feminist movements have engaged in systematic campaigns for "*despenalizacion social*" or "social decriminalization" of abortion, a broad framework that is deliberately oriented toward cultural change. In Africa, the activists I spoke with described a multilayered social and cultural landscape, in which abortion was stigmatized, but even more, feared for its health risks in an environment where access to medical care was often limited—one reason for African activists' approach to abortion through the more expansive frameworks of sexual and reproductive health.

When we step back from questions of law and enforcement, a larger landscape comes into focus in which risks emerge from social and institutional contexts more than from law. Some of the contextual factors seem obvious: socialist governments are perceived as safer than center-right ones and the anonymity of a large city provides protections that don't exist in smaller, more conservative places. Other factors, particularly those shaping how much individuals disclose about their activism, are harder to predict as they arise from the dynamics of a particular location or relationship. Some forms of visibility are protective, especially at the organizational level, while others may bring risk. How activists balance openness and discretion has to be understood in relation to the surrounding social and cultural dynamics.

This chapter began with a brief discussion of openness and alliances across movements as forms of protection, but these coexist with protective caution around the actual physical locations for work. All the collectives and NGOs in this study were, and are, highly visible on the internet as an intrinsic element of their work, and many of them have also posted or distributed flyers, stenciled phone numbers, and otherwise done what they can to help people with unwanted pregnancies get the information they need. However, when it comes to a physical location, the collectives don't have a publicly visible snail mail address and the formal offices of NGOs are not always easy to find. In Mexico City, I walked back and forth on a side street, just off a major commercial avenue, looking for an address that did not appear to exist. Finally, feeling like a stupid gringa, I called the person I was there to meet; she told me their office was in a building behind a gated metal fence that had no address on it—which I had stood in front of in frustration for some minutes, unable to see a street number or a buzzer. In Kenya, the public address for the local NGO bafflingly leads you to a museum, where there is a garden connected to the organization—and the private address took me to a small road with two or three wooden gates in a well-off area outside Nairobi. The taxi driver was also baffled and went up to a security guard, who pointed us toward one of the gates where I finally noticed a small, quite discreet logo. In Nigeria, on the other hand, the taxi driver confidently took me to a clearly marked building with the organization's name prominently displayed at street level in the bustling neighborhood. All organizations are visible in contexts that enable communication, but the majority have relatively low visibility in more material contexts, where the risks of harassment or assault can take physical form.

In relation to communication, the emphasis on visibility is a kind of surface layer over structures designed to manage a combination of security and access. All collectives and NGOs strive to be as accessible as possible to persons with an undesired pregnancy, but things become more complicated after the initial contact. The hotlines are the most open, and will provide information to anyone, although they have to manage "fake" callers out to harass or entrap. As one hotline activist in Chile described,

> We were getting these hoax calls . . . For example, a caller will say, "Hi, I want the information," and after we've given it they'll start on where are you from, where are you based, where can I come and see you.

The accompaniment groups need to screen somewhat more carefully since they engage in more individualized and extended contact both electronically and in person. For this reason, there is typically some form of multistage process for accompaniers to connect with people looking to end a pregnancy. When I was in Argentina in 2016, not yet doing research, the Socorrista groups I spoke with around Buenos Aires each had a public telephone number that was widely available as well as a private one that was only given out after an initial conversation, and other accompaniment groups seem to use similar strategies for balancing accessibility and security. After an initial screening process, collectives may hold a meeting with a small group of people seeking abortions to talk about their experiences and the abortion process together as a way to reduce stigma and isolation. Organizations also hold public informational workshops about abortion, women's health and rights, and related topics, which usually focus on sexual health and rights instead of exploring individual experiences. Public meetings entail the greatest vulnerability to harassment but also offer the protection of high visibility and draw attendees who are interested in the intended program of events. In contrast, the meetings for and interactions with people with undesired pregnancies all occur after some screening has taken place, reducing the risks of exposure, harassment, and/or threats for everyone involved.

One of the most important factors shaping risk, across all my research locations, was the nature of the town or city where someone lived and worked. A large city offers some anonymity and, at least in the twenty-first century, a certain level of cosmopolitanism that can accommodate a diversity of values and ways of living. Smaller cities and towns may be more conservative and, perhaps more important in regard to abortion, completely lack anonymity. The accompaniment network in Ecuador includes the capital city of Quito, the midsize city of Cuenca, and Esmeraldas, a small, extremely religious city on the coast that was founded by Africans who escaped a Spanish slave ship. The Quito collective could hold small workshops and operate with an assumption of privacy, largely based in anonymity, while the collectives in both Cuenca and Esmeraldas worked from the assumption that anonymity was impossible and therefore privacy had to be carefully created. One of the Cuenca activists described the lack of anonymity:

> [Cuenca] is a small city . . . We might be recognized by a person we'd accompanied and sometimes, like, she'll try to avoid us—crossing

> the street to the opposite sidewalk, like not to see us. It shows that shame is still a very powerful factor.

Even in Argentina, a place of relative openness, activists in smaller towns and cities sometimes had difficulty forming connections with local health care workers, which are important for getting a woman respectful medical attention when needed (especially with second-trimester abortions).

There are other situations where anonymity is impossible and ongoing relationships can provide security to counterbalance the risks of being known. Community workers in Kenya described the importance of having roots in the communities where they worked, and the protection that came from being known and respected. As one woman put it, describing an altercation with the family of a woman whom she had aided,

> The [woman's] sons were threatening me. Now, after consulting with the community, the community said if they come and get you, just tell us . . . So, for me, it's just that I was backed by the community people. Or else, you see how the sons could have come physically and attacked me. So, being an activist is also not a very easy job, you see?

This quote illustrates how being known can create risk—the woman's sons know the worker and where she lives—as well as the safety of being a valued member of the community who will be protected.

Questions about the risks of being open about one's activism, and the potential consequences of this, were a thread that ran through almost all my interviews and informal conversations. For the staff of the movement NGOs, of course, this was more straightforward, although in their home communities many found it easier to say they worked for a women's health NGO. As one Kenyan hotline worker put it,

> I say okay, there's all these things you need to do. But of course, they don't know I work with the hotline, but I still give them the number . . . I don't have to let them know. People think I'm supposed to know who is behind the telephone.

For those who make their living outside the movement, however, decisions were less straightforward and were affected by their occupation as well as the dynamics of a particular workplace. For activists whose work was distant from their movement lives, the question of disclosure was often relatively low-key. One woman in Ecuador, for example, had been employed in the tourist industry for a decade or more, and was the senior manager of a travel agency when we met in Quito; she was relatively open at work, but it did not seem to hold much weight for her one way or the other. Another woman worked in a library, and again the question of who knew what about her outside commitments seemed more a matter of convenience in relation to her schedule than anything else.

The question of disclosure was most acute for professionals, who often had to manage the complexities of actual or potential overlap between their professional work and their activist commitments. A lawyer in the Dominican Republic, for example, took for granted that her legal work on abortion was well known to her colleagues but was much more discreet about her involvement with the local accompaniment collective. A Chilean whose research and professional life was divided between Buenos Aires and Santiago described the Argentinian universities as places where everyone wrote their dissertation on their abortion activism—but in Chile, that would make it difficult or impossible to get an academic job. In 2017–19, the Chilean activists I met who had PhDs generally described working for international NGOs or the government, or perhaps had temporary teaching positions. A European activist living in Chile had a full-time position at a university, and she understood that she needed to be very careful about what she revealed about her movement connections. I was introduced to two feminist public health professors, one very senior, who both saw the SMA activists as radical and relatively distant from their own activist circles. In contrast, a graduate student easily introduced me to a member of a new abortion network, MisoPaTodas, and I gradually met a number of PhD students involved in SMA collectives, although their movement ties were not necessarily visible in their emerging professional lives. Among those who had a history of government employment, there was a shared agreement that the women's division of the government was the most difficult place to work as an abortion activist; the only person I spoke with who had been set up and then fired for known movement connections had been in the Chilean government's women's division.

There is a group of professionals for whom there is no separation between their work lives and their activism, which brings its own potential risks. For some lawyers employed in human rights and social movement contexts, their connections to SMA are at the center of their occupational lives, and this can bring a kind of public visibility that is very different from that of a law professor who publishes on abortion and feminist legal theory. The same is true of senior administrators in NGOs that work on SMA, who do not have the luxury of information control in most situations.

The media create distinct forms of contextual risks for these NGO administrators, since a certain amount of media exposure and communication are intrinsic to the education and advocacy side of their work. For example, in 2018 a photo and article on the front page of the major Polish women's magazine drew attention to the work of the four women known as the "Abortion Dream Team;" one of them, the director of an international telemedicine platform, was advised not to attend a meeting in person immediately afterwards, and another one is, at the time of writing, facing charges for assisting a woman with an abortion. In another example, after a senior staff person at a Mexican NGO participated in an interview and debate for a Mexican television program, she was subjected to a barrage of violent, personal threats from far-right and religious activists, most of them based on her disclosure during the program that she had had an abortion herself. In both of these examples, the risks from visibility in the media were fundamentally linked to the power of an increasingly global antiabortion movement.

Gender, Sexuality, and the Global Far Right

The expansive presence and power of the global anti-feminist and anti-LGBTQ+ far right was visible throughout the research for this project, starting in the first week of my trip to Chile in 2017. I was in a small café in downtown Santiago—one that became a favorite spot for me over the next two years—and heard a lot of shouting outside, then saw people running past carrying signs. Many of us in the café went to the door to see what was happening, and saw the bright orange CitizenGo "gender bus," with its anti-trans, pro-traditional-gender message. The shouting came from a mix of supporters and counterprotesters, all pursued by the Santiago police. I followed the crowd out of curiosity and then had my first introduction to protest control, Chilean-style: there was an old modified tank with a powerful water "gun" in the turret that indiscriminately sprayed protesters (and anyone else in the vicinity), most of whom dodged into doorways and opened umbrellas until the hose-down stopped. In this case, no one was injured and the whole thing had a performative element, though the tank's presence pointed to the Chilean police's capacity for violence.

While abortion (and LGBTQ+) rights appear on the surface to be struggles that take place country by country, the focus on national laws and court decisions obscures the global nature of antiabortion organizing. Of course, this book maps a global feminist movement for abortion that challenges the global far right—but there are sharp differences between these movements in funding and institutional power. The movement for SMA consists of grassroots, regionally anchored networks that are linked globally to each other and with strong international feminist organizations in order to share strategies, resources, and support. The global anti-feminist/anti-LGBTQ+ far right, however, has significant money and institutional power. While these right-wing "pro-family" institutions largely operate at the level of law and policy, their presence and global spread has also been associated with an increase in targeted harassment of feminist and LGBTQ+ activists, including both symbolic and physical violence.

There is a cohesive politics—and a concrete network of financial and political connections—among the right-wing, anti-feminist/LGBTQ+ organizations active throughout Europe, the Americas, and sub-Saharan Africa. This is the politics that unites Putin's Russia, Orbán's Hungary, the government of Poland, and the US Republican Party, among others, and is based in a White nationalist ideology. It may seem contradictory to say that organizations active in Africa and Latin America have ties to White nationalism, but it is clearly true in relation to anti-feminist/LGBTQ+ networks. Two of the largest are the global umbrella organizations CitizenGo (of the gender bus) and the World Congress of Families (designated as a hate group by the Southern Poverty Law Center), each of which brings together many other organizations that have significant reach on their own. In 2018, the board of CitizenGo included members from the right-wing Spanish organization Hazte Oir ("Make Yourself Heard"), the World Congress of Families, and several right-wing Catholic and evangelical organizations.[7] The World Congress of Families, for its part, brings together a broad array of prominent right-wing and evangelical Protestant organizations, and has been linked to White supremacist groups in the United States and Europe.[8] Both CitizenGo and the WCF have been directly and indirectly involved in supporting anti-abortion campaigns and organizing throughout Latin America and Africa, often in alliance with local evangelical Protestant churches. Many of these churches also have ties to US evangelicals, and have imported an aggressive, at times violent, antiabortion politics along with a neoliberal pull-yourself-up-by-your-bootstraps theology.[9]

The linked growth of evangelical Protestantism and the international anti-feminist/LGBTQ+ far right has shifted the risk and security environment for SMA organizations across Latin America and sub-Saharan Africa. CitizenGo has a significant presence in Nigeria and Kenya, and was named by staff at organizations in both countries as part of the opposition that they face. Kenya has been a particular focus of right-wing organizing, first during the process of constitutional change around 2010, and then afterwards, in response to the implementation of the new, progressive constitution that supports women's rights. In Latin America, the rapid growth of Protestant evangelical churches, with their intensely conservative gender and family politics, has become an even greater threat to women's and LGBTQ+ rights in some ways than the Catholic Church. One of the hotlines in Chile was harassed by an evangelical church, although the harassment didn't prevent the hotline from operating:

> One evangelical church sued us for something or other; the case was dismissed, the prosecutor declared it inadmissible because it wasn't—they were accusing us of an offense [but] there was nothing that went beyond the framework of information, it was just informative.

The power of the evangelical right can be seen most obviously in Brazil, but it extends to other countries as well, and generally brings a more immediate, confrontational political style than the

Catholic Church's institutional power. In 2018, the annual July 25 abortion march in Santiago was attacked in two different places, once along the route of the march and again at the end, which had never happened before.

In the middle of the march, a group of men from a right-wing organization, Movimiento Social Patriota, held up a banner and called for the sterilization of march participants. As I marched past them with a group carrying a banner for the abortion hotline, they sloshed buckets of liquid and oddly shaped white, glistening objects across the line of march—which I was told later were animal intestines. There were reports of fires being set in the streets behind and around the march, and at the end, as the crowd dispersed, three women were stabbed by masked attackers, reportedly while the police looked on. While this was an exceptional level of direct violence, it reflects the escalation of the threat to activists that has come with the expansion of an extreme right-wing politics linked to evangelical churches with ties to the United States and global far right.

While physical attacks seem to be rare, digital attacks are a common form of right-wing antiabortion harassment globally. All the organizations I spoke with reported increases in online harassment, including hacking and cloning of websites, and a corresponding increase in attention to digital security practices. Hotlines have always managed a certain amount of harassment through abusive phone calls and, somewhat more subtly, "fake" callers who try to draw activists into forms of communication that could be considered criminal, such as direct advice or counseling. Over the past ten to fifteen years, digital technologies have become more sophisticated and widely available, and forms of online harassment have similarly become more complex and organized.

Digital Tools and Digital Security

The relationship between the movement for SMA and digital technologies is a little like that between fish and water; the tech is so integrated that it can at moments be hard to actually *see*, and not just take for granted. When I first connected with one of the online telemedicine platforms, in 2017, I was concerned that I would be doing most of the interviews online and that I would not be able to really experience their work environment. Then I came to understand that online is precisely the environment in which they work, every day. Sitting in an apartment, logging in to an online system, scheduling team meetings on Jitsi or BlueJeans, checking on the email traffic for a language team, and picking up communication with women wherever a colleague left off. They were doing it long before COVID, and the pandemic did not directly change the organization of work for most of the telehealth platform staff, although it did affect the issues facing the people who contacted the platform. The hotlines and accompaniment collectives also do much of their work with people seeking abortions by email, phone call, and text, although they generally meet in person on a regular basis. Because most digital communication involves sharing information that is at best stigmatized and at worst illegal, learning digital security has become as central to day-to-day activist work as learning the WHO protocol for medication abortion.

Digital security is generally framed as a set of technical practices, but in my conversations with SMA activists it became clear that it also involved attention to matching communication modes and content. At the design level, there are extensive protections against hacking built into websites and online systems, and activists have a strong preference for open-source software over commercial packages. One of the women involved in setting up the first online telemedicine platforms is an artist with ties to

European feminist hacker networks. She has continued to play a central role in thinking about digital security within the movement, although she is quick to say that local experts are always essential when doing security design and training, since they will understand the lived contexts and conditions better than any outsider. I heard about the use of Virtual Private Networks (VPNs) to ensure secure access to online systems, and anonymous browsers that don't leave traces or save search histories. There was also a significant emphasis on ordinary "hygiene" practices that do not require extensive training, like not using WhatsApp or public Wi-Fi for any communications that should be secure, and setting messages to automatically erase on encrypted apps like Signal or Wire.

The question of matching communication mode and content is relatively nontechnical, although it does require thinking about the nature of different digital environments. The key factor driving the choice of communication modes is, unsurprisingly, the extent to which the message is intrinsically public or potentially private, and what kind of communication can occur through each medium. For example, generic information about medication abortion that is not directed toward any particular individual can be shared on social media; but if someone posts a personal question in a reply to your generic post, then further conversation needs to move off social media and into a more secure form of communication. Facebook and Twitter are great for raising awareness, general education, anti-stigma messaging, and advocacy, where their public nature as a broadcast media is most useful—but that same public quality makes them completely inappropriate for any communication that could carry personal risk. For example, the Facebook page for Miss Oprostol, in Mexico, has a "Call Now" button, and the Facebook profile picture for one hotline in Kenya has contact numbers that someone can call. The US group, Plan C, has links to webinars and online publications with information about SMA and how to be an "SMA buddy," as well as links to sites with phone numbers for direct communication. The general message of "here is how to get information or help" is very different than active, individualized attention to a particular person's questions and situation; the first is safe on social media but the second should only be done through secure email or text in order to avoid exposing everyone involved to potential risks.

Holistic Security as Theory and Practice

As noted in the beginning of this chapter, the overall framework of "holistic security" (or *seguridad integral* in Spanish) comes from efforts to ensure the safety of human rights defenders, especially in the Global South. Holistic security brings together all the arenas of threat outlined above—the legal, societal, and digital realms—and adds a key additional focus on the social, emotional, and psychological elements of doing this work. At the most basic level, someone who is experiencing significant stress, anxiety, and feelings of isolation will—in addition to being vulnerable to burnout or stress-related illness—be at elevated risk for lapses in digital or other forms of security practices, potentially putting others at risk as well as herself.

The centrality of self-care within holistic security practice runs counter to the internal cultures of many social movements, which often develop implicit ideologies of strength, sacrifice, and impossible levels of dedication. An activist in Brazil who has become deeply committed to self-care as a security practice described the way she used to think and feel:

> When you are a feminist activist, you want to break with the position of submitting to men, patriarchy, and whatever. And then suddenly, you realize that you have completely surrendered yourself to feminism. You got yourself in a position that is like, "Okay. So, I don't

> want to dedicate my life to men. But I'm completely dedicating my life to activism." And you just don't learn to say no to things, even when you feel in your body that you won't be able to do it. I got to this point where I would never say no to anything, to any task no matter if it was inside the organization or with coalition partners. And this was absolutely devastating physically and mentally. It was not like something big happened—it was just like an accumulation of lots of little things.

Similarly, a hotline activist in Ecuador described a collective ethos of emotional control and self-sufficiency in the early days of the hotline:

> We didn't used to have such a process of self-care, but now after ten years it's sort of necessary . . . [Before], everyone coped as best they could, they had to keep answering the phone because it was their shift, it was like, here's another woman who needs the information straight away, wipe your eyes and pick up the phone again. So now, I feel it can be a much more loving process because we're in a different place for sure, so we can sustain it, that's been really great, in fact, building these networks and strong mutual bonds that enable us to keep going.

The accompaniment collectives have developed a powerful discourse on care and supported self-care in relation to women having abortions, but it can be challenging to apply that philosophy within an activist collective where different ideals and needs can at times conflict.[10] The quotes above from Brazil and from a hotline point to the ways that self-care has to be a shared practice within a collective, and to the idea that setting limits can feel like it conflicts with the needs of the movement. Accompaniment demands even more time and attention than answering a hotline, and as a member of the Ecuadorian collective Las Comadres said,

"We work courtesy of the networks" because the demands of an accompaniment require support for everyone involved. Over the long term, this work comes to shape the lives of activists in ways that go far beyond questions of security and self-care, which is the focus of the last chapter.

SMA activists have to manage multiple forms of emotional and social stress that come with their work. I will explore these in more detail in chapter 7 on long-term involvement in the movement, but the management of stress as an element of security is an essential part of a holistic perspective. As described in the preceding sections of this chapter, activists manage legal ambiguities, persecution by law enforcement, harassment and sometimes physical attacks by far-right movements, and political and cultural shifts, both supportive and oppositional, in the broader society. In their personal lives, they may confront some isolation related to their work, including the need to control information about their activism around family members, coworkers, and even some friends. And the work of answering a hotline or accompanying an abortion can bring its own stress and pressures, as the activists I've quoted above describe.

For these reasons, the emergence of a framework for security that includes self-care was described by activists as transformative as well as challenging, especially for those working in the most high-risk environments. It has proven essential to the maintenance of long-term work in Brazil and other high-pressure contexts, where respecting one's own and each other's limits are essential. In the experience of one Brazilian activist,

> When we talk about self-care, it's often all about the individual. And what we try to do with groups is to bring things to the level of the collective . . . For example, if we have a breakdown in this group from someone who doesn't want to be part of it anymore but doesn't

> say why, we can go back and try to understand what was making her so stressed. [With one woman, we found out] it was picking up the phone. And nobody ever realized that. Okay. So, picking up the phone, it's feeling very stressful. So, who [else] can do that?

One aspect of the power of a collective lies precisely in the balancing of roles, and the knowledge that a task that is difficult for one person may be easier for someone else. While the language of holistic security emerges from distinct locations and is more common in the Global South, the more general concept of respecting each other's limits and the need for emotional and psychological support inside activist spaces has become more widespread across progressive movements. In the United States, for example, Black Lives Matter has characterized self-care and mutual love as radical acts that further the collective struggle. For the feminist activists I met, the only way to balance the threats and risks with their commitment to long-term engagement in the movement was through a commitment to this holistic vision. In other words, valuing the full humanity of oneself and one's *compañeres* helps to keep each other safe and sane. In some circles, that's called "holistic security."

5

We Have Become the Experts: Scientific Research, Medical Protocols, and Movement Knowledge

The Socorristas are committed to learn and disseminate knowledge, which advances at a fast pace and is firmly grounded in the experience of abortion accompaniment. Their research and reflections are progressively opening towards finding new ways to help women in the abortion process, far beyond the mere appropriation of knowledge derived from the medical sciences. (Second Trimester Medication Abortions: A Feminist *Socorrista* Study)

The process of sharing knowledge—about medication abortion, how to run a hotline, strategies for accompaniment, digital and holistic security—has been a theme running through the first half of this book and is a central form of political action within this movement. This chapter will explore how knowledge—especially scientific and medical knowledge—about SMA is developed as part of the political work of the movement.

For those who are theoretically inclined, the analysis in this chapter draws loosely on the sociology of science and critical science studies to explore the production of scientific knowledge as a social—and socially embedded—process. Scientific knowledge emerges from multiple locations, not just laboratories—and even in a lab, the development of knowledge through observation, experiment, and analysis always takes place within larger social and institutional systems that affect what is considered important, how experiments are designed, and how analyses unfold. The movement for SMA has relocated these practices of observation, data collection, analysis, and even publication of research results, into the hotlines and accompaniment spaces where activists and people self-managing an abortion engage in solidarity-based direct action together. This merger of science and feminist direct action has changed global public health knowledge and policy.

Health movements typically advocate for increased scientific attention (and funding) to specific diseases or conditions, but in the late twentieth and early twenty-first centuries, a growing number of movements began to engage in the direct development of scientific knowledge as part of both political struggle and community action. Environmental justice activists have done this through documenting the impact of environmental damage on communities, as well as efforts to remediate or prevent environmental harms.[1] HIV/AIDS activism offers multiple examples of community-based knowledge development as part of political organizing: for example, the "buyers' clubs" during the 1980s brought experimental drug regimens to people with HIV and AIDS, and then collected data from members about their experience with the medications. HIV/AIDS activists also ran community-based clinical trials (e.g. ACRIA), and harm-reduction activists collaborated with epidemiologists to validate the efficacy of street-based health interventions—activist-scientific work that is still ongoing. In the '60s and '70s, women's health activists built a woman-centered body of knowledge about women's health through the processes of observation, documentation, and adaptation within self-help groups, consciousness-raising groups, and feminist health collectives and workshops, which have clear analogues in the work of SMA collectives, especially in Latin America.[2]

Through much of history, knowledge about women and reproduction was developed through observation, practice, and sharing information in community contexts, largely among women.[3] As was described in chapter 1, reproduction was medicalized as part of the larger project of formalizing and professionalizing medicine in America and western Europe, and the argument that physician-controlled abortion would be safer than the hazards of unregulated "quacks" played a key role. In the 1960s and '70s, when abortion was still largely illegal in the United States and western Europe, feminist activists of the second wave began to demedicalize abortion and knowledge about women's reproduction in self-help groups, but this nascent demedicalization was largely derailed by the legalization of abortion and creation of feminist medical clinics that functionally remedicalized both knowledge and practice. The advent of medication abortion has reopened the linked processes of demedicalization and the creation of autonomous knowledge.

SMA activists throughout the world engage with scientific knowledge production in three overlapping ways, each of which contributes to the demedicalization of both abortion and the creation of knowledge about abortion as an element of women's lives. First, activists without formal medical training have taken ownership of teaching each other and people seeking abortions how to use medication safely and effectively to end a pregnancy in both the first and second trimester. (The latter is particularly significant given the medical and legislative marginalization of abortion after twelve to fourteen weeks.) Second, many SMA organizations study medical protocols and then adapt them to the particular circumstances within which the organization works, refining their knowledge through ongoing processes of observation, analysis, and further adaptation. Through this, they create their own autonomous protocols that integrate standard medical practices with the realities of demedicalized community settings—and then share these adapted protocols with other SMA collectives. Third, some SMA organizations have developed collaborative relationships with feminist epidemiologists to gather data about the safety and efficacy of these activist-created protocols, validating them with mainstream scientific methods and thus shaping the scientific literature.

Within the movement for SMA, activist engagement with the development of scientific knowledge is part of their commitment to solidarity-based action. For Las Socorristas of Argentina, for example, their commitment to recognizing the full range of situations facing people with unwanted pregnancies led them to extend the gestational age for which they would accompany abortions, and they have developed the skills and knowledge necessary to support the abortions that need to happen.[4] This process has involved extensive collaboration with epidemiologists to evaluate outcomes, and to document and explore activist practices of knowledge development as well as the experience of accompaniment itself.[5] As a result, SMA activists know more about second-trimester medication abortion than many doctors, and have higher success rates for completed abortions without surgical intervention.[6] This speaks to the lived complexity of solidarity as a set of practices that involve far more than the moments of interpersonal interaction or "showing up" but extend into the diverse forms of work that precede, underlie, and enable the ability to meet someone wherever they are, even—or especially—when that exceeds the boundaries of standard WHO protocols.

The Authority to Teach

The word "demedicalization" explicitly directs attention to the absence or rejection of medical authority, the idea that medical professionals are not necessary for the treatment and care that a condition requires. The ongoing normalization of telemedicine abortion can obscure how radical it was not so long ago, especially in the United States, to trust women to have an abortion at home rather than a clinic, even though telemedicine still maintains medical authority; in contrast, there is a direct negation of authority when people with no medical training master technical knowledge and teach it to others. In Kenya, prior to the start of the hotline, there was resistance from local authorities to the idea of teaching women how to safely use medication. As one Kenyan activist said,

> [There was] a lot of no, we can't trust women with that information . . . Like, women have no capacity to actually administer and conduct an abortion on their own . . . They'll not take the medicine as they're supposed to.

In the United States, where hotlines and accompaniment are not (yet?) visible options, the struggles have largely been over asynchronous models of telemedicine, in which someone completes an online form and communicates with a provider by email or text message. This model of care comes from the international platforms, like Women Help Women, and is based on trusting women to provide the necessary information, understand instructions, and manage pills at home. The assertion of medical authority can sometimes take on a protective tone of ensuring the quality of care. As one of the founders of Plan C told me,

> Synchronous Telehealth was still very medicalized. Right? It still had ultrasound, it still had bloodwork, it still had all of that. The model we were proposing was the [international telemedicine] model where you don't need to have that testing . . . That was what was causing the pushback [from the FDA].

At a National Abortion Federation conference in 2017, a panel on harm reduction and abortion was met with a significant amount of negative concern about "not going back" to a pre-*Roe* world, effectively conflating the self-use of medication with the methods used in the 1960s and early '70s (often symbolized by a coat hanger) and positioning the clinic as the only safe location for abortion in the twenty-first century. This model of abortion safety through medicalization opened up in the United States during the COVID pandemic and then in response to the recriminalization of abortion in many states, but it can still be seen in legal arguments that focus on medical legality rather than full decriminalization.

In the earlier chapters, I described how technical training, whether on the use of medication or cybersecurity, initially came from Europeans or North Americans and then was adapted regionally as local activists took over the process. In this chapter, the distinction between Global North and Global South recedes, since none of the activists are formally trained medical personnel. While the founder and director of Waves/Web is a doctor, the staff who worked with local activists around setting up hotlines starting in 2008—and who have continued this work as Women Help Women—are people without formal medical training, demonstrating that medical certification is not necessary to develop expertise or to train others.

When movement activists take on the authority to learn and share medical knowledge, they transform the understanding of what needs to be taught and how skills interconnect. An activist-designed training combines formal medical protocols with the knowledge of how to run a hotline, how to respond to people who call, and how to provide technical information in a way that's useful to callers. A hotline manager in Lagos described their process:

> I train our staff and also regional[ly] to other counselors, other positions that want to establish a hotline . . . first of all, how to accept a call. And then, after that, the misoprostol.

One of the founders of the first Chilean hotline said,

> [Waves and Ecuador] came to train us . . . They shared the Ecuadorian hotline's experience, and also explained their experience of organization . . . In other words, our discussions had a political dimension and an organizational dimension as well as being a course [on medicines] and an overall acquisition of knowledge.

It's important to recognize that the work of a hotline or accompaniment collective integrates the technical knowledge of the use of medication with interactional skills needed to respond to people in stressful situations, all framed through a feminist political analysis. The Chilean quoted above went on to provide training to a new collective in Peru:

> We went to train the women, and also to teach telephone skills. It was two separate things, like some women invited us to hold workshops on how to abort using pills, so they could use that information, while others were interested in being telephonists.

This democratization of information is part of the radical demedicalization of SMA and the movement to support people with SMA. Activists have learned the formal step-by-step procedures and then adapted them to be usable within the actual contexts in which they support people seeking abortions. This does not contradict the legal framework of the right to information, but it does highlight the lived complexity of what it means to share information. To choose a small, pragmatic example, information about the expected amount of bleeding and levels of pain has to be communicated in ways that make sense to an ordinary person in the middle of a stressful situation, such as defining a potential hemorrhage through the number of maxi pads used in two hours. Activists all over the world have created short, easy-to-use, step-by-step instructions that translate WHO protocols into something accessible to ordinary people with minimal formal education. While this practice began as the province of community "experts" like hotline staff, the process of creating and sharing accessible materials has been further decentralized and dispersed among a broad array of feminist (and other) actors. As an activist in Chile put it,

> At one time [the hotlines] were the only place to discuss abortion, the sole source of information. And then everything changed and feminist women emerged all over the country, eager to share the information.

It's also important to recall, from chapter 1, that women in South America were teaching each other how to use misoprostol to abort long before there was an organized movement.

There are analogies here to other health movements where activists have also taken on the authority to learn, translate, and teach medical information. For example, overdose prevention is a harm-reduction strategy that teaches drug users and other community members to use (and carry) naloxone, a medication to reverse opiate overdoses commonly used by EMTs and emergency room personnel. Carrying naloxone and knowing how to use it enables those most likely to witness an overdose to stop it and save someone's life. Harm-reduction activists first began to demedicalize naloxone in the late 1990s, handing it out to syringe-exchange participants and teaching them how to use it, and then adapted their protocols for use as a more powerful opiate, fentanyl, came into circulation and caused overdoses to skyrocket throughout the United States. One of many examples of community ownership of medical knowledge around HIV/AIDS is what came to be called "treatment education" in the late 1990s. Community service providers translated technical medical information about medications and treatment protocols into ordinary language that could be understood by people with HIV/AIDS regardless of their education level, enabling people to advocate for themselves and take ownership of their own treatment regimens. This practice spread through global activist networks and was particularly important in low-income populations (and countries), and among those with reduced access to medical care.

The movement for SMA not only asserts that women can safely and effectively use medication on their own but goes a step beyond that to claim that education, self-assessment, and decision-making are fully within the purview of pregnant people and nonmedical community members. The international telehealth platforms, hotlines, and accompaniment collectives ask women who contact them how long they have been pregnant but do not require an ultrasound as a precondition for women to receive information and support. The information shared with those who call or email includes contraindications for medication abortion, such as having an IUD, and guidelines for identifying normal versus problematic levels of bleeding, pain, and fever. The structure of SMA and activist support presumes that people without formal medical training can not only learn the standard protocol for medication abortion but also assess the process while it is underway, evaluating what is taking place in relation to what is expected. When women reach out to activists during an abortion for reassurance or to ask a medical question, everyone involved assumes that the activists have the knowledge and experience to work with someone to accurately assess their situation—including when things are not going as expected (as with the story in chapter 3 of the hotline worker managing the situation of a woman who initially said she was early in a pregnancy when in fact she was in the second trimester).

While, technically speaking, activists are sharing information, they are doing so in ways that significantly challenge the boundaries of medical authority, precisely because they go beyond literally sharing the WHO protocol. Activists who work with pregnant people develop knowledge and experience in ways that are analogous to the experience of a medical professional, a midwife, or a doula. The assumption that women can accurately assess their own situation and safely apply and interpret medical information is part of what elicited the resistance to asynchronous models of telemedicine from the FDA, as well as other authorities. The movement for SMA demonstrates every day that women can effectively combine medical information with knowledge of their own bodies to safely care for themselves and each other.

Demedicalized Protocols

A medical protocol outlines scientifically validated procedures for the use of medication, or for a medical treatment/procedure, but the implementation of a protocol, of course, has to be adapted to each patient and context. Medical education would be much more straightforward if high-quality care just involved following a step-by-step list of instructions with no need for assessments, interpretations, and adaptations to the lived reality of a particular human being and the immediate context of care. Thinking through what should not be changed and what can be modified is one of the challenges of demedicalization—of moving medical protocols out of clinical contexts. For example, needle exchange programs teach safe, sanitary injection hygiene to people who inject drugs in places that include alleyways and abandoned buildings. Needle exchange staff and participants worked together to develop strategies for hygienic injection in extremely non-hygienic spaces, and the combination of improved injection practices with access to sterile supplies has dramatically reduced abscesses and other infections among injection drug users. SMA activists described a similar process of studying, adapting, and sharing medical and activist protocols, particularly when launching a new collective, starting to accompany second-trimester abortions, or expanding their work in any way.

The collective that founded one of the Chilean hotlines went through an extensive process of self-organized study in addition to being trained by Waves/Web and a member of the Ecuadorian collective. For example, they found and downloaded a manual on the obstetric uses of misoprostol from FLASOG, the Latin American federation of obstetricians and gynecologists, as described by one of the hotline founders:

> There was this very good manual . . . to complete abortions, designed for a medical context. It explained how to complete an abortion where there'd been a spontaneous but incomplete miscarriage, how to use misoprostol to induce labor, how to use misoprostol postpartum. It was super-thorough . . . and we studied it, it was one of the documents that taught us the protocol.

In relation to SMA, the use of the medical word "protocol" has expanded to include aspects of the experience of SMA that go beyond the technical details of using abortion pills. This is visible in the way the hotline activist above talks about studying a comprehensive manual on medication abortion as a way to "know the protocol"; the manual covers far more than just instructions on the pills, and the study of the manual speaks to the actual breadth of knowledge useful to those who support self-managed abortions. She went on to say that the manual disappeared from the website of the organization a few months after they downloaded it, which seems related to a larger pattern throughout the region of governments and professional associations reducing access to misoprostol as knowledge about its use as an abortifacient became more widespread. A number of hotlines have produced their own abortion manuals, which are of a very different nature than those of an association of obstetricians and gynecologists. Unlike medical ones, the feminist manuals address multiple aspects of the abortion experience and larger sociopolitical context, with a particular emphasis on reducing stigma and isolation by interweaving personal stories with political analysis and practical instructions.

The accompaniment collectives engage with the question of protocols in a more complex and ongoing fashion than hotlines. One of the founders of the Ecuadorian accompaniment group described an extended process of study and adaptation through which the collective developed their own accompaniment protocol prior to formally launching the group:

> In 2014 our initial protocols were with reference to Las Libres, the Socorristas, the Fondo María . . . because we were all friends, we were close already. But of course we looked at their protocols and [selectively] merged them, this bit is great, so's that, and in light of our own context we'll do it this way. So it was a fusion, understanding our own context in its difference from the others.

The description of creating "our initial protocols" implicitly references an ongoing process of reflection and adaptation that goes on within accompaniment groups, as group members share experiences, further develop their practice, and engage in dialogue with other activists and collectives. As another member of the Ecuadorian accompaniment group put it, "We're in constant touch with each other . . . they refer cases to us, we refer cases to them, we consult on difficult issues, some are experts in certain topics."

Accompaniments are generally documented, at least in handwritten notes, to facilitate this practice of collective learning and knowledge development. Las Socorristas in Argentina have formally collected some demographic and outcome data at least since 2014, with annual accompaniment statistics published on their website. While other groups don't necessarily self-publish data, they do collect it in the course of their work and, as will be discussed more in the next section, a number of SMA collectives and NGOs have collaborative relationships with feminist epidemiologists.

The growing practice of second-trimester SMA has moved accompaniment collectives, including a few hotlines, into a higher level of engagement with autonomous knowledge production. When activists began to accompany second-trimester abortions, in the mid-2010s, there were published medical protocols on second-trimester medication abortion, even with misoprostol alone, but formal medico-scientific knowledge in this area was less developed than for the first trimester. For example, the WHO has formal protocols for second-trimester SMA, but those seem to have developed simultaneously with, not preceding, the work of activists, particularly in Argentina. In 2015, the data published by Las Socorristas on their website indicated (successful) second-trimester abortions, and a member of Women Help Women described being invited to do a presentation on second-trimester medication abortion with Las Socorristas the following year. A study of second-trimester accompaniment produced internally by the Socorristas, published in 2018, noted that activists were often more knowledgeable about second-trimester medication abortion than their allies within the medical system.[7]

Activist knowledge, in other words, is crucial—both to the broader community and to the scientific and medical world. Legal restrictions on abortion, combined with strong stigmas, mean that doctors may learn little or nothing about abortion within their professional training. For example, a gynecologist in Chile who supported women with abortions, and directly provided them whenever legally possible, had to intentionally seek out training in abortion care outside South America. When Chile finally lifted the complete ban on abortion left behind by Pinochet's dictatorship and allowed abortions in very limited cases, a bilingual US doctor was brought in to provide training to Chilean physicians on abortions in the second and third trimester. It's worth noting that in the United States, abortion techniques were not a mandatory part of OB-GYN training programs even before the *Dobbs* decision, a fact that demonstrates the power of stigma (and fear of the Christian right) over comprehensive medical training.

The greater level of uncertainty around second-trimester abortions, and the need to develop autonomous knowledge about them, as opposed to simply adapting established medical practice, was clear in the ways activists talked about this work. From one activist in Ecuador:

> We've been brought together over second-trimester abortions, which we don't all handle; on our network as well, only some of us do that . . . The same happens in other cities and countries, they don't all handle second-trimester cases. That's why we got these groups together [regionally] to address that, we share, we recognize, I don't know, we even tell each other how we use the various medicines. The protocols are different.

She went on to say that some of the Ecuadorian activists who are experienced with second-trimester abortions were "accompanying" Colombian activists who had begun to do this work, which evokes a very different interpersonal process than when activists "train" new people. It was clear in multiple ways that the activists who accompany second-trimester abortions were actively working together to develop and share knowledge about how to do this in a way that is simultaneously safe, effective, and feminist.

When scientific knowledge is understood as socially produced and located, as knowledge based in both a social and technical interpretive structure, then the material produced by SMA collectives can be seen as generating forms of scientific knowledge. The manuals, protocols, and other materials produced by SMA collectives intentionally make visible the perspectives and values shaping their work and the relationship they see between the situation in which an abortion takes place and the actual process of performing it. (Of course, professional materials also contain perspectives, values, and assumed contexts, though these are typically presented as "proper procedure" and/or "good clinical practice.") There are many earlier examples of how social movements have shaped medical practice: in the 1970s, feminist knowledge about abortion that was developed in social movement spaces shaped the new norms for professional practice in the US clinics that emerged following *Roe*.[8] Similarly, harm-reduction practices developed by and with people who inject drugs have come to reshape the practice of addiction medicine in certain ways, such as incorporating overdose prevention within drug treatment, an activist protocol that initially challenged treatment ideologies and practices.[9] In the twenty-first century, SMA networks are developing knowledge and practice within community spaces in active dialogue with more traditional sources of scientific and medical knowledge. This brings the power of demedicalized and democratized knowledge and care into the more traditional spaces of science and medicine in ways that can help pregnant people everywhere.

Working with Scientific Researchers

Movement collectives and NGOs conduct research related to SMA in a few different ways, from informal surveys to formal collaborations with epidemiologists to test the safety and efficacy of hotlines and accompaniment as abortion care. In the United States, two different SMA organizations described periodically conducting informal surveys via their community email list to assess network needs and guide planning. The Kenyan NGO described research collaborations with multiple partners, including a study of the impact of the US global gag rule, as well as work on SMA, which they presented at reproductive health conferences.

The visible connections with external research institutes largely involve epidemiologists, who ask the kinds of research questions that are directly useful to the movement, questions focused on the demographic characteristics and social circumstances of the people contacting a hotline or accompaniment group and the outcomes of the abortion itself. This kind of data helps a collective evaluate their own work and think about ways to improve it. There was a similar relationship between syringe exchanges and epidemiologists, particularly in the 1990s but continuing today, in which the work of epidemiologists was directly relevant to furthering the goals and work of the movement. (The potential contributions of a sociologist interested in social movements—me—seemed less clearly useful to SMA activists, even among those who participated in this project.) Before exploring activist engagements with science, however, it would be useful to step back to look at research on SMA in general, which will provide some background for thinking about movement/research engagements.

Public health and medical research on medication abortion and self-managed abortion has followed a few different paths, some traditional and others less so. At the most mainstream or traditional end of the spectrum, there is a body of work on the effectiveness of Mife and Miso, or Miso alone, to induce abortion under clinical conditions at different gestational time periods. This is the work that informs guidelines from professional associations and the WHO, although the WHO also draws on a wider array of work. Research on this end of the spectrum focuses on what is currently considered "medical abortion," meaning medication abortion under clinical supervision, rather than self-managed medication abortion, which takes place without clinical supervision. Anything that takes place under clinical supervision can be studied in a relatively straightforward way using traditional recruitment methods and research design, all of which fit within the institutional logics of mainstream clinical care.

Research on SMA is methodologically more challenging, since by definition it takes place outside of clinical settings and is done by people who may not want to be found by scientists (or anyone else). In public health, this is a fairly well-known research design issue, since investigators are often interested in studying stigmatized situations and issues—but the questions underlying most public health research are quite different than the questions involved in testing the outcomes of a treatment protocol. For example, if you want to know the frequency of an experience then you need a random sample that is representative of the overall population of concern, and you ask all study participants a series of questions to find out how many people have had the experience in question. For example, a study of the frequency of SMA in Texas in 2015 found that somewhere between 1.7 percent and 4.1 percent of all women in Texas eighteen to forty-nine years old had tried to self-induce an abortion, typically NOT with medication.[10] A similar study of women in the United States as a whole calculated that 7.1 percent of women try to self-induce an abortion at some point in their lives, also generally not with medication.[11] To put those numbers in perspective, about 25 percent of American women report having had an abortion at some point in their lives, so it is possible that a meaningful proportion of women who have abortions may at least try to self-induce.[12] These kinds of studies indicate how widespread SMA may be—a goal of traditional public health research—but don't examine the safety and efficacy of it, with or without support from a feminist SMA collective.

The central issue with SMA, to make explicit what may or may not be obvious, is that in order to test a treatment, you need to collect data from enough people who have used the treatment to be able to say something systematic about the outcomes. When both the treatment and the condition being treated are socially stigmatized and legally criminalized, then recruitment for research can be difficult. This is particularly true in relation to abortion, which may be relatively common across the lifespan of a large proportion of people but infrequent in any one person's life. For research design, frequency matters and so do social networks, since it is easier to find people who do something regularly, in part because they probably have friends who also do "it" (whatever "it" may be). For example, to choose another stigmatized and criminalized issue, people who regularly use illicit drugs need to acquire their substance of choice and typically know other users as well as dealers, all of which makes it possible to find and recruit them through social networks. The need to recruit study participants is one of the reasons why, as a society, we know more about people who use a drug habitually than people who use it occasionally; it's easier to find the habitual users than the occasional users. Overall, the situation with SMA is closer to that of occasional drug users than habitual ones. There are studies of SMA with women recruited word-of-mouth through social networks, such as a Chilean study of university students, but this results in very limited sample sizes.[13] More problematically, some studies have recruited women through medical settings that provide abortion or postabortion care, a practice that may exaggerate the frequency of negative outcomes because data has been obtained from a location where people are more likely to go when SMA didn't work as they had hoped.

To continue with the research analogy on illicit drugs, the most effective form of HIV prevention with injection drug users is syringe exchange/distribution programs and harm-reduction strategies in general. Syringe exchange is a community-based intervention developed by drug users and AIDS activists to prevent the spread of HIV. Activists and epidemiologists worked together to evaluate the effectiveness of this autonomous health strategy, which was created entirely outside of clinical settings.[14] Initially, a small group of public health research professionals built relationships with emerging (not necessarily legal) syringe exchange programs to assess the effectiveness of their work and learn more about the challenges faced by the people exchanging syringes. These collaborations formed during the height of the War on Drugs, when profound societal stigma and political hostility towards illicit drug use made syringe exchange deeply controversial; as a result, studies of these programs needed to use traditionally recognized methodologies so their results would be scientifically impeccable. For example, studies that recruited participants at syringe exchange programs commonly used a technique that generated a random—and therefore representative—sample of participants at each site. There is a radical solidarity in the scientific decision to use mainstream methodologies, working in criminalized contexts, to test the outcomes of completely demedicalized health protocols, treating autonomous activist protocols with the same respect applied to a traditional clinical protocol.

Much of the research over the last fifteen years validating the safety and efficacy of SMA has been done in collaboration with international telemedicine platforms and SMA organizations, each of which supports hundreds or thousands of self-managed abortions every year. The international telemedicine platforms are designed in ways that are relatively compatible with the basic frameworks of medical and epidemiological research. Women who contact the service fill out a "get started" intake form with information about the pregnancy and their health, and then communicate in an ongoing way via email with the staff of a help desk. In effect, a kind of abbreviated medical record is created that can easily have any identifying information taken out; this basic data can then be used for certain kinds of analyses, which is a fairly common strategy in quantitative studies of medical treatment. For instance, these records have been used in studies evaluating the outcomes of SMA with telemedicine, which found results comparable to medication abortion in a clinical setting, and used to examine the reasons why women seek abortion through telemedicine.[15]

This work has been central to demonstrating the safety and efficacy of SMA and played a role in the expanded authorization for telemedicine abortion in the United States during the COVID pandemic. A doctor with one of the international platforms believes the work they do could have significantly more of an impact on medical research and practice if the documentation challenges could be overcome:

> You cannot imagine the medical abortion cases we're taking with this organization, . . . cases which are officially considered contraindicated . . . We are still doing them, counseling medically for the woman, giving her the support, and they are passing through these cases successfully . . . [In practice] you choose between offering counseling services to a woman or documenting the details of the previous case . . . [Research] shouldn't create a burden for the help desk.

The research on SMA through hotlines and accompaniment groups reflects a radical solidarity and long-term investment in building trust between the movement and feminist epidemiologists, analogous to the relationship that developed around syringe exchange. These collaborations emerged out of an interest among both activists and (a few) feminist epidemiologists to evaluate the protocols and support models used by hotlines and accompaniment collectives. The initial studies involved two or three activist groups but have since expanded, in both the number of collectives engaged with research as well as the ambition of the research projects to address both the science and the care of SMA. An early scientific article in 2016 looked at the characteristics of first-time hotline callers to argue that hotlines did not just reduce harm but in fact provided high-quality care.[16] The understanding that activist support for SMA provides high-quality care regardless of legal conditions has consistently been at the center of this research, as in a recent article explicitly arguing that mainstream medicine should learn from the movement.[17] Another article examined accompaniment of second-trimester abortion as a form of community-supported care, challenging individualized definitions of "self-care" by reframing it as a communal or shared experience.[18] One of the more methodologically impressive examples of this shared work was a study that recruited women who contacted abortion accompaniment groups in Argentina and Nigeria and followed them through completion, demonstrating results that were comparable with those in a clinical setting.[19] In a conversation, one of the scientists on this project said that, in fact, the outcomes with Miso alone were better with activists than in clinical settings, in part because activists allowed the process to unfold at its own pace instead of referring someone for a surgical abortion if the medication didn't work in a set time frame.

Public health research on controversial practices and contexts, such as SMA or syringe exchange, faces significant scientific as well as social scrutiny. This elevated scrutiny underlies the importance of using mainstream methodologies in order to produce work that is technically unimpeachable, though radical in its conclusions. The scientists who do this work understand the complexity of the scientific as well as societal context for their work—and if they should forget it, they are likely to be reminded. In 2018, I attended a feminist abortion conference in New York City where there were two presentations on SMA in the second trimester, one from a representative of an online telemedicine platform and the other by an epidemiologist working with an accompaniment collective in South America. The structure of each presentation was fairly traditional, although both women clearly understood that their material would be seen as provocative (and enjoyed it). Even in this explicitly feminist, abortion-oriented scientific conference, the level of discomfort in the room was palpable: the idea—never mind the scientific evidence—of second-trimester medication abortion outside of a clinical context clearly made a number of the feminist doctors and scientists in the room feel anxious or even threatened.

Second-trimester abortions are treated as marginal and undesirable even among abortion providers, are more difficult to obtain, and are considered more complex medically as well as socially. The commitment, knowledge, and experience developed by activists who accompany second-trimester abortions is thus significant, and the shared work between activists and researchers to validate the safety and efficacy of these demedicalized, community-created protocols constitutes a meaningful form of political solidarity in its own right. The horizontal structure of these activist/epidemiologist teams combined with the use of traditional scientific methods intrinsically treats the knowledge, experience, and demedicalized abortion protocols of feminist activist collectives as equivalent to those of licensed clinical practitioners—and does so publicly, both in the scientific literature and on the conference circuit.

The existence and effectiveness of these long-term, growing research collaborations also speak to the importance of understanding SMA as a social movement, with an expanding and diverse membership that can include feminist scientists as well as frontline activists. The teams engaged in shared scientific work have gradually expanded through movement networks to create projects with sites on three continents, from Latin America to Indonesia to sub-Saharan Africa. Activists in each location share strategies and abortion protocols before coming together in a joint project, and recognize each other as doing the same work in different parts of the world. Some of them had already met at one (or both) of the global SMA activist gatherings that took place in 2016 and 2018. The global meetings and the multinational studies speak to the shared values, understandings, analytical perspectives, and direct-action strategies that are defining characteristics of a social movement, and make it possible to develop a research team across thousands of miles and in multiple languages.

While this book focuses primarily on the work of collectives and NGOs that support people seeking abortions, the movement itself is broader. As discussed in the chapter on risk and technology, there is a network of lawyers that spans the Americas from Canada through the Southern Cone to develop and share legal rationales for action, identify potential legal risks and strategies for managing them, and when necessary provide immediate, non-theoretical legal support for women who have had abortions and the activists who support them. There are doctors, psychologists, and other care professionals who form an expanded network around SMA collectives to provide support as needed to women before, during, or after an abortion. And there are epidemiologists who have built sustained relationships with frontline activists to study, evaluate, validate, and further develop their work as abortion practitioners who enable safe abortions in demedicalized community contexts—despite stigma and criminalization.

6

We All Work Together: Building Activist Networks from the Local to the Global

> *[At international conferences] we were hearing countries that had even more restrictive laws than ours having hotlines, we were like oh, we could do that. We think this is doable. So, at one of these meetings, I think it was in 2012, we started to have that conversation. We really want to start a hotline. So, we reached out to Women on Waves and told them we want to get trained on how people start hotlines . . . So, we organized the first training. It happened here in Nairobi . . . So, now we started. When Nigeria was ready to start a hotline, they said guys, come and share with us your experiences. Let us know. Since we helped you launch, what has happened so far? How are you getting calls? How are you getting women to know? How are you navigating the law? It is safe? And now we started to go with Women on Waves . . . we went and supported Nigeria to launch theirs, Malawi, Tanzania. We went and did the first training in Burundi.* [Kenya]

The idea that relationships and interpersonal connections are central to getting things done, at work as well as with your neighbors, can seem simultaneously obvious and invisible. If I want to reserve a room for a university event, I talk to the department administrative coordinator before I fill out the form because, as every college professor and most graduate students know, the department administrative staff are the people most able to get things done regardless of the official channels. Then there's the neighbor who has keys to probably half the apartments on our floor, who is happy to water plants or feed pets when needed and handles all the vet visits for the elderly woman at the end of the hall who can no longer carry her pudgy cats. My phone contacts include people who train activists in civil disobedience and others who can share information about self-managed abortion, a friend who works for a union and so knew a good labor lawyer when someone else needed one, and even a couple of teenagers looking for babysitting jobs. Everyone has their own version of these interpersonal maps, also known as social networks, and we use them to keep life moving along.

When I was in graduate school in the 1990s, the meaning of the phrase "social networks" had not substantively changed, at least within sociology, for decades. It certainly didn't yet mean Facebook, and telephones were still only used to make phone calls. In 2007, I published a paper on drug-user networks and the circulation of syringes that could still assume that these networks functioned through direct human interaction as people met up with other people to distribute sterile syringes. All of this has changed, and any sociological discussion of networks in relation to social movements (or anything else) has to consider the multidimensional nature of our contemporary understandings of networks and the meanings of the phrase "social network" in particular. And, of course, interpersonal and organizational networks now use all kinds of digital communications, of which online social networks like Facebook are only a part. In looking at the social networks (in the old sense) of the global movement for SMA, I will largely use the phrase "movement networks" to avoid confusion with today's multiple meanings of "social networks," and with the understanding that movement networks encompass relationships between individuals as well as between organizations.

Networks play an essential role in the emergence and ongoing work of social movements. As described in earlier chapters, the first hotline in Ecuador was created by a feminist youth organization that shared the story of their launch; a video was circulated among feminists by email, and members of the Ecuadorian collective did a workshop at a long-standing regional feminist conference. A feminist HIV organization in Africa looked for information on abortion to share with their members and was directed to the Amsterdam-based staff of an international telemedicine platform, who then came to Kenya to provide training in medication abortion. And so on.

Social movements do their work this way, using any communication platform that's available. I used to attend Passover seders with a woman who had physical limitations from childhood polio. During the civil rights movement's Freedom Summer in 1964, her disability kept her in off-site movement roles, which meant, on one occasion, that she spent an entire night on the phone calling a list of police stations repeatedly to try to find an African American activist who had been arrested. None of the stations admitted to having him in custody, but he was released alive the next morning—perhaps in part because someone in Chicago made it clear that these small-town police stations in the South were being watched.

All social movements build their work through relationships among individuals and between organizations, but it is particularly important for movements working in criminalized contexts. When I did research on drug-related harm reduction, my long-standing visibility as an activist enabled me to engage relatively easily with unauthorized or otherwise marginal programs, without having to first prove that I understood how to conduct myself at a sex worker outreach site or during a parking lot meeting to move cases of syringes from one car to another. My early efforts to connect with SMA movement networks required both some form of personal connection and a willingness to have the informal conversations that build trust before moving on to interviews. Once, I sent an email to a hotline email address to introduce myself and ask for an in-person meeting; this got an autoreply with instructions for the use of misoprostol for a first-trimester abortion, and, sometime later, a very terse two-sentence email with instructions to meet someone in a small plaza near a metro station. (The second email did not come while I was in the city in question, so I had to turn it down.) In contrast, when I had plans to be in Buenos Aires in the very early stages of this project, someone with whom I had a distant connection introduced me to an Argentinian activist, who then forwarded an email from me to a listserv of activists. A few days later, two different collectives in the larger Buenos Aires area reached out to me to schedule a time to meet and then hung out for more than an hour over tea and maté. In each example, an email from me went to a general address with a request to meet and talk, but it was the one that traveled through movement networks to an in-house listserv that elicited a response that recognized me as a *compañera* rather than an outsider.

These movement networks are essential for creating bridges within and across movements and regions. As I described in the introduction, I was introduced to SMA as a concept through an all-day meeting organized by a lawyer who works at the intersections of reproductive justice and drug-related harm reduction. She then introduced me to one or two SMA activists in the United States with ties to transnational networks and organizations. Movement ties can be found in less obvious places as well; a Chilean American friend and academic colleague introduced me to a friend of hers in Santiago whose wife turned out to know a young woman who was part of a then very new SMA network in Chile. I had two or three Skype calls with the young SMA activist before her group decided they weren't comfortable working with an outsider—and I later came to understand that the organization had probably existed for less than six months when I had contact with them. The project evolved to take a more transnational perspective in part through my developing relationship with a European organization with global connections (WHW) that is widely trusted by activists on the ground across countries and continents. In many situations, being introduced by the right person is crucial to opening up opportunities—but this dynamic can be particularly strong in relation to social movements that engage in (sometimes illegal) direct action, which depends on internal trust.

The movement for SMA has formal, named networks that link organizations nationally or regionally, and also densely woven informal networks among activists who know each other and among organizations that do similar work. The formal and the informal interact over time, with formal networks emerging from informal connections. In Latin America, collectives form ongoing networks within each country, and the dense connections across collectives throughout the region sometimes coalesce into something more formal when needed. In Africa, the MAMA Network initially brought together women's health organizations that were already in contact with each other but has since formalized, developing a process for new organizations to apply for membership. There have been two international meetings that brought together hotline and accompaniment activists from across the Global South, although these appear to have strengthened regional networks rather than led to the creation of a formal transnational network of frontline SMA activists. There are also long-standing collaborative transnational relationships between organizations based in North America and Europe and those in Latin America, Africa, and parts of Asia. For example, Mexican organizations have ties south to the rest of Latin America but also north to the United States—which expanded significantly after Texas banned all abortions after six weeks (SB8) and Mexican feminists began to accompany US women during SMA. Movement networks also cross movements, as in my experience with links between harm reduction and SMA, and the connections across different forms of feminist accompaniment in Latin America around gender violence as well as abortion. SMA movement networks are, above all, part of larger feminist movements with their own interpersonal and interorganizational ties.

In the rest of this chapter, I explore how movement networks operate at national, regional, and transnational levels. I realize that regional networks cross borders and therefore are, by definition, international but they differ in certain ways from the networks I consider "transnational." In chapter 2, I introduced the geography of my research by describing some of the historical and contemporary patterns that shaped the development of the movement for SMA within different parts of the world, and those patterns underlie the different regional networks discussed in this chapter. Regional networks share certain historical experiences and contemporary socioeconomic challenges—such as the common experience of dictatorship and resistance in Latin America or the relative marginalization of sub-Saharan Africa within global economic systems. In addition, regional networks often reflect long-standing organizational relationships, as with the MAMA Network, and include organizations that do similar work and often collaborate, as with the forming of hotlines across South America around 2010. Transnational networks are less likely to share common historical experiences—or share them from different sides of the power spectrum, as with Europe and its former colonies—and bridge organizations that engage in different kinds of work or work in very different social and cultural contexts. I largely approach these as connections between collectives/organizations although I understand very well that there is often little distinction between personal and organizational networks, especially in the informal context of national and regional organizing. In chapter 7, I'll move from this more general discussion of movement networks to consider how these networks shape the lives of long-term SMA activists.

Local and National Networks

Each collective or NGO exists within an ecology of relatively local organizations and people who share work, resources, perspectives, and commitments. For example, in chapter 3, I described how hotlines and accompaniment groups recruit new members through their personal friendship networks, gradually expanding outwards with each successive wave of recruitment. The connections that sustain an SMA organization resemble a web more than expanding circles, with linked SMA collectives at the center, professionals who directly support SMA in one set of threads extending outwards, and other threads that involve a range of feminist organizations and activists. The networks are somewhat different in Africa than in Latin America because the African hotlines have paid staff and can serve an entire country, which means they are not part of a local nucleus of SMA organizations although they have connections to supportive professionals and other feminist NGOs

Across Latin America, SMA collectives are connected at the national level, generally as a single organization with local branches, and activists move between local groups as their lives take them from one city or town to another. In Argentina, the Socorrista website lists sixty-four accompaniment collectives, all part of the same umbrella organization but each with its own contact email and phone number. The greater Buenos Aires area has several individual collectives, which makes sense given the magnitude of the population and geography involved. The relationship among geographically distinct collectives can vary over time: in Chile, the hotline began as one organization across multiple cities and then subdivided into formally separate groups, while in Ecuador the hotline has remained as a single entity. Similarly, the accompaniment organization in Ecuador has local collectives in different cities but understands itself as one whole rather than separate parts. In Mexico, the situation is more dispersed legally and organizationally; abortion is regulated at the state level rather than federally, and organizations that provide support with SMA have varying levels of connection to larger networks. For example, there are established NGOs in both Mexico City and Guanajuato that are well integrated with formal and informal regional networks of hotlines and accompaniment, and smaller collectives that work locally but may have little outside connection.

The local and national networks that surround SMA organizations reflect the local social and political contexts shaping abortion and feminist activism. In Kenya, the organization that houses the abortion hotline works on an array of issues surrounding health, HIV, and traditional knowledge. Their networks are quite diverse but also periodically affected by the US global gag rule, as discussed earlier. The Nigerian NGO anchors its work within a larger framework of women's empowerment, which brings it into conversation with groups concerned with education and economic opportunity as well as sexual and reproductive health. In both Kenya and Nigeria, local networks initially emerged during trainings with community health workers, leaders of youth groups, and women's groups around medication abortion and other aspects of sexual health and rights. As a Kenyan activist described it,

> We started this work of where do women get their information? . . . So we started to train these women in communities, in places of fetching water, cleaning, getting information out there.

The extended circles around organizations in both Africa and Latin America include professionals that can provide legal and psychological support as well as medical support when needed. In addition, all the SMA organizations that I had contact with also participated in larger policy-oriented coalitions and activist campaigns to decriminalize abortion, end gender violence, and other key feminist struggles.

One of the distinctive things about emerging SMA networks in the United States is their current level of disconnection and dispersion, although that may have changed by the time this book is published. The United States has begun to reverse decades of progressive laws that had expanded civil rights, something that was once unimaginable. In practice, the erosion of voting rights through a mix of direct restrictions and indirect strategies (e.g. gerrymandered districts) has been integral to the loss of access to abortion as well as the resurgence of anti-trans and anti-LGBTQ+ legislation. Like in Mexico, the legal status of abortion post-*Roe* varies dramatically from state to state in the United States, as do the political contexts and therefore the legal pressures confronting activists. The slow but steady spread of knowledge about SMA in the United States accelerated significantly under COVID, when going to any kind of medical facility suddenly felt like a health risk, and then continued to expand as Kavanaugh and Barrett were appointed to the Supreme Court and Texas banned abortion after six weeks (SB8). The release of the *Dobbs* decision transformed the discussion of SMA, and the use of medication took center stage as a strategy for maintaining access to abortion in the face of an ever-growing wave of state-level restrictions. By the fall of 2022, there were multiple networks that either directly supported and enabled SMA or incorporated information about SMA into a larger set of health issues, but there was relatively little connection or communication across networks. This may prove to be useful and even become a deliberate strategy, given the extent of state-by-state legal variability and, at least as important, the depth of politicization and criminalization of abortion throughout the country. The politicization of abortion, or other aspects of bodily autonomy such as gender identity, significantly shapes the ground on which activists operate as they provide community level support, and US activists must now build state-level and national movement networks and strategies while navigating a political spotlight. As in Mexico, some are doing this in the context of regional and transnational connections, while others have few ties outside their own local area.

Regional Networks

Regional networks develop within the parameters of a relatively shared culture, history, legal environment, and language, and involve routine forms of ongoing collaboration and communication. This can be seen in patterns of inclusion and development within regional networks: Portuguese-speaking Brazil is something of an outlier within Latin America, less integrated but not excluded from movement networks, but Guyana (an English-speaking country on the Atlantic coast of South America) appears completely outside the abortion-related discourse of "Latina America y el Caribe." Patterns of colonization leave behind common legal frameworks and cultural as well as linguistic patterns; African countries that were colonized by Britain negotiate a different legal heritage than those colonized by France, and the MAMA Network in sub-Saharan Africa initially emerged in English-speaking Africa with the gradual inclusion of Francophone countries a few years later. Regional networks engage in mutual support, share resources of various kinds, develop and refine forms of direct action, and work together around common political-legal challenges. The emerging Mexico–US networks fit with this tradition of direct action and shared resources, despite lack of a common culture and language—although it's notable that much of the south-north collaboration began with Latin American immigrant communities in the southern and western US.

When I first expressed an interest in regional and transnational abortion networks, activists in Santiago suggested I talk to women who, I quickly discovered, worked for NGOs with international connections, such as one funded by a German foundation and another linked to International Planned Parenthood. In the world of NGOs, there are formal regional linkages between organizations that work in similar areas and attend the same conferences, and most local activists I talked with assumed that someone (at least a gringa) asking about networks was interested in the NGO world. The SMA collectives in Latin America participate in national and regional networks of feminist NGOs and have been very involved in the political struggle to legalize abortion, referred to as *La Marea Verde* (the Green Tide). Shared work directly on SMA, however, such as developing protocols for second-trimester abortions, happens through separate SMA-specific networks, in part for the protection of both NGOs and SMA activists.

Interestingly, the web of dense, often informal connections among activists in different countries was a taken-for-granted part of hotline or accompaniment collectives, and these connections were not necessarily defined as "networks." When someone would describe how a newly forming group would reach out to others for support and I would ask, "How did you know them?" there was often a slightly perplexed look and variations on, "Well, we know the same people." The word "network" (*red* in Spanish) was often interpreted as applying to organizations and to connections that had been formalized enough to be named; for example, an activist in Valparaiso explained that there was a network of hotlines in the early 2010s, which meant the hotlines organized formal meetings and identified themselves as a network. Before that and after the official network disbanded, they communicated constantly and met informally but did not label themselves as a "network." I learned to ask questions in a different way in order to find out about informal friendship-based networks as well as formal, self-identified organizational networks.

The line between organizational and personal networks can be particularly blurry at the regional level, which reflects the way networks evolve within and across movements. It often took some back and forth between me and the people I interviewed to bring out how friendship networks form over years of shared political work and facilitate connections across many miles and borders. For example, a Chilean activist reflected on how an activist from Mexico came to meet with her group in Valparaiso:

> Because these are feminist connections. One compañera from the organization was doing a doctorate in Mexico. And she hooked up with a compañera from Las Libres, and we . . . took advantage of how this Mexican compañera was going to go somewhere else but she came to South America and we got her to pass through Chile.

Regional conferences, of course, play an important role in forming the relationships that lead to shared work on SMA. A group of Kenyan activists recalled the origins of what has become the MAMA Network in sub-Saharan Africa:

> Speaker 1: The way it was formed, it was during a reproductive health, and I think, an abortion conference . . .
>
> Speaker 2: The 28th of September is [international] safe abortion day. So that day was the biggest celebration when it comes to safe abortion. On that day those organizations decided, what if we created our own group? . . . Just an informal group of activists who wanted to share the same issues, the same situations, the same legal context.
>
> Speaker 3: [It was all] grassroots organizations because they are the ones who are at the forefront of dealing with the women. We know

> that the big organizations are there. But when we talk of the real impact, it's the community organizations.

It shouldn't be a surprise that artistic subcultures, particularly musical ones, also provide environments that both create and sustain relationships among movement activists. There was a distinct thread of feminist punk music that ran through the networks of SMA activists in their thirties and provided some cross-cultural reference points for women from different countries. For example, the music connection helped a Mexican activist who went to Chile for graduate school to get connected to movement work. I also heard joking references to a car trip across the Andes involving activists from two or three countries that was fueled by a punk soundtrack. And in the early 2010s, a Chilean activist who was part of an Augusto Boal–inspired Theater of the Oppressed regional network spent some time in the Guatemalan highlands doing theater-based political education, where she ran at least one workshop on abortion in response to interest and need among young women in the community.

Across regions, formal networks are built from pre-existing informal ties among organizations. Activists' description of the MAMA Network as coming out of "an informal group of activists" who met at conferences has parallels in Latin America, where regional feminist conferences serve as key meeting points, along with other reproductive rights events and radical student networks. A key difference between these two regions, however, is the extent and duration of the formalization of networks. In sub-Saharan Africa, the informal group of grassroots NGOs described above that began on September 28, 2016, is now a formal, funded network of thirty-five-plus NGOs with two coordinating organizations and a process through which new groups can apply to join. In contrast, the Latin American hotline network formed in 2010 or 2011 as a way to share strategies and support new abortion hotlines, and then gradually faded away. The contrast between a formal, funded network of African NGOs and the more flexible networks of Latin American collectives reflects the difference between NGOs and collectives as much as anything else; the work within the networks appears more similar than the structures.

One of the central functions of regional networks, whether formal or informal, is to share knowledge and resources through various forms of mutual aid. A new network of SMA accompaniment collectives began to form in 2018, which an Argentinian activist described as emerging from years of interaction and support:

> Meetings are not the starting point of these formations or coalitions, but they do seek to, well—set the stage for the possibility of a network of accompaniers throughout Latin American and the Caribbean . . . We'd already, like I said, been coordinating, consulting, helping each other out, sharing materials . . . and above all sharing our viewpoints, you know? So out of all that comes the political impulse for get-togethers that aspire to intervene politically in a region plagued with constraints and considerable penalization and criminalization.

A Chilean offered more insight into what this looks like in her description of a trip to Lima to train and support an emerging collective in Peru, using the idea of accompaniment to convey the experience of mutual aid among activists:

> I spent about a week in Peru . . . with a woman from the Ecuador hotline. While we were there we consolidated our contacts and joined in various activities; we attended the launch of the hotline, but we also accompanied the Peruvian compañeras in their own activisms.

A Nigerian described her experience of receiving support from other activists during the launch of a new hotline:

> The Kenyan [hotline] helped us. In case of anything, we need the help from them. We do call them. They even give us connection to other organizations, which are working with the same thing we are doing.

Interorganizational support goes well beyond a moment, or even a week, of training and extends into ongoing alliances, initially to support new projects but also in a horizontal fashion among experienced activists. Mutual aid comes through personal networks as well, particularly among those who move between countries with different levels of accessibility to misoprostol. A woman whose work takes her between Chile and Argentina used to do some accompaniment but now largely helps behind the scenes:

> Me and a lot of other people travel with pills . . . not for big organizations, but more informally. I had a friend . . . and I told her like, "I have this amount. I'm giving them to you particularly," but I know that she's part of a network.

Europe and the United States have long had feminist organizations and networks that facilitate abortion-related travel, which is a somewhat different form of regional cooperation than the SMA-focused networks of Latin America and sub-Saharan Africa. Women in the Global South also travel for abortion, especially among the middle and upper classes, and this will probably increase in Latin America as more countries legalize abortion. While women have sometimes traveled long distances to access abortion care, the associated costs and stresses put this out of reach for most—one of the main challenges facing US abortion providers and activists now, after the fall of *Roe*. The emerging map of abortion laws in the United States means that a person seeking an abortion in the Midwest and much of the South has to travel considerably farther than a Polish woman seeking an abortion in a neighboring European country.

Geographically and politically, given the US legal and policy structure, the United States resembles a region more than a country in some ways. Abortion funds have helped women travel to clinics for many years, including across state lines, and Mexico has long offered access to affordable medical care and pharmaceuticals for those who live near the border and can safely cross. Activists in Mexico began openly supporting women in Texas in September 2021, and are expanding their cross-border accompaniment at least through the southern United States. Misoprostol is available over the counter in Mexico, as are many other medications, and pharmacies line the border region to provide a wide range of pharmaceuticals to North Americans without a prescription and at lower cost than a few miles north. Pre-*Roe*, feminists in California developed relationships with abortion doctors in Mexico, and SMA activists are working together to directly facilitate access to medication and digital accompaniment. We can assume there will soon be abortion travel across the Canadian border as well. The cross-border collaborations among Mexican and US feminists to support women in the United States seem more regional than transnational, given the direct-action focus on enabling abortions and the flow of technical knowledge and assistance from experienced SMA activists towards newer ones.

Transnational

The networks I consider transnational encompass significant differences of geography, language, culture, and often, though not always, power and resources. The primary transnational networks that I know of run between the Global North and the Global

South, although there were two global hotline meetings (that I am aware of) centered on frontline activists that created some informal transnational South-South networks. Transnational SMA networks somewhat disrupt the dominant assumptions about the flow of knowledge between South and North: these relationships are deeply collaborative rather than hierarchical, with all involved bringing significant and valued areas of expertise. This is particularly true for the lawyers' network, where the Latin American lawyers bring extensive experience with the legal issues surrounding SMA in relation to both the work of activists and the dynamics of risk for people self-managing an abortion in different societal and legal contexts. It's important to note that my research focused on activists, rather than donors or foundations, and if I had focused on the latter, it's likely that I would have found a more hierarchical structure than the peer-to-peer connections among frontline activists. This does not mean that SMA networks are horizontal in an ideal way, given the profound imbalances in global distributions of power and resources between countries and hemispheres, but nonetheless the dynamics among activist organizations from different regions and hemispheres are very different from those between a northern funder and southern grant recipient.

Transnational North-South activist networks play a few key roles for SMA organizations in the Global South, some of which are short-term and others ongoing. A crucial short-term but recurring role has been to assist with technical assistance of one kind or another, either through brief trainings or support with grant proposals. Chapter 1 described the role of a core group within Women on Waves who provided the initial training on medication abortion to the first hotlines in Latin America and for groups in sub-Saharan Africa, followed in each case by ongoing consultation through the initial phase of a hotline or another form of outreach. This core team went on to create Women Help Women as an organization that was built around demedicalization and long-term connections with local partners, and that has been able to sustain relationships that combine collaboration with occasional technical assistance. Ongoing collaborations vary significantly depending on the group and the context but include enabling access to medication, connecting an emerging collective with experienced local or regional activists, and conducting occasional shared projects. Technical assistance may take the form of assistance with writing grant proposals, facilitating connections with other transnational NGOs or with SMA organizations on other continents, and bridging local organizations with international conferences, particularly those in the Global North. A Nigerian activist who now works comfortably in global settings described her early experience: "[The conference] we went to . . . people from all over the world. So, it is not very easy to fit in appropriately, even the language, the speech, and everything."

When I was in South America from 2017 to 2019, there were regular trainings taking place on digital security and the development of the holistic security framework described in chapter 4. These trainings offer a valuable illustration of how transnational networks operate within the global movement for SMA, and the centrality of shared expertise between the Global North and Global South in circulating knowledge. The initial awareness of security came from Women Help Women, who had recently gone through their own internal security training process, and a series of trainings were done throughout Latin America by the Institute for Gender and Technology. While the technical information may be taught by feminists from the Global North, the process of adapting it to a specific location must be interactive, as described by a woman living in Amsterdam: "It's a process, like the trainers learn, also, from the trainees, and the trainees learn from the trainers, so it's a mutual exchange." She went on to emphasize the impossibility of reliance on outside experts when using a more holistic approach to security:

> [It's important to] do the work with local trainers, local security experts, first of all, because I don't want to be the White European going to Africa, telling people what they should be doing. Second of all, it would not be complete training because I'm—even if I can read about this, I'm not living there, and I cannot assess for 100 percent. I cannot fully understand the picture.

Political activism is done within a particular context, and the development of genuine security in that context cannot come through external expertise but has to be a shared creation among those with technical, cultural, and social knowledge as well as deep familiarity with local practices. The northern activists I spoke with understood clearly that all forms of technical knowledge and training, including on digital security or protocols for SMA, must be part of a mutual exchange that is based in knowledge of local conditions. This idea is also reflected in the voices of two activists—the first was in Ecuador, where feminist collectives were undergoing a security training process when I was there in 2019, and the second in Mexico. The first quote also makes clear the breadth of national SMA networks and how they interact transnationally:

> Women Help Women has embarked on a process involving several [abortion] hotlines. And recently, as part of that, we were talking about holistic security . . . We linked up with some twenty-two collectives all concerned with abortion. (Ecuador)

> With regard to digital security, now, we took part in the institute's training initiatives . . . focused on feminist organizations . . . and we learned about various tools. One of our contacts is a woman in Mexico . . . who works precisely on internet safety. (Mexico)

Another area in which shared work requires genuine and deep North-South collaboration within transnational networks has been the development of scientific knowledge of SMA as a truly demedicalized, autonomous practice in community settings. As discussed in more detail in chapter 5, there are sustained relationships between activists working on the ground in different parts of the world and research teams in the Global North. The majority of the studies with hotlines and accompaniment collectives have been done by members of a particular feminist research group, at Ibis Reproductive Health, that has built relationships with activists and collectives in Indonesia and Africa as well as Latin America. As with technical assistance training, these are not simple, vertical relationships in which American or European epidemiologists set up shop at a location and gather data to analyze and publish unilaterally; these projects develop collaboratively to answer questions of interest to both activists and scientists, and the resulting publications include authors from all locations. This approach to research is not unique to this movement, but this is definitely not the dominant approach within public health. It is important to recognize that the creation and development of scientific knowledge flows in all directions through these transnational networks, among people with varying levels of formal education and with varying points of entry to the shared work.

With the exception of conferences, which are discrete but often repeating events, these transnational networks are simultaneously stable and fluid, organizational and personal, long-term and focused on a particular piece of shared work. They are largely informal in nature, except when there is a shared grant or specific project, like a research study, that formalizes a relationship for a period of time. For example, Women Help Women worked on some shared grants with African organizations, particularly around the creation of the MAMA Network as an official entity, although the grant was held by the African NGO. Otherwise, these transnational networks have similarities to the informal networks that organize relationships among collectives across

Latin America, with long-standing personal relationships that blur the boundaries between the individual and the organizational.

Women Help Women functions as somewhat of a transnational network in itself, in both structure and staffing, in addition to being part of larger transnational networks and regional European ones. In the first chapter, I described the basic structure of Women on Web during its early days, and then of Women Help Women as an interlinked structure of NGOs, with each NGO incorporated in the country with the best laws for a particular area (pharmacy regulation, decriminalization of abortion, financial factors). As the core work of the telemedicine platform is all online, the staff can be diverse geographically and linguistically with online communication platforms as their "conference room" and English the lingua franca. An administrator responsible for managing an array of internal operations at WHW commented wryly on the intrinsic challenges of communicating about complex, sometimes emotionally laden issues in a language that is not native to the majority of staff members. In my first visit to Amsterdam, in 2017, my notes from an initial conversation indicated that staff lived in at least fifteen countries across eleven time zones, and it has no doubt grown in the intervening years.

This dispersed staff of WHW embodies the transnational networks of SMA activists, especially given that the majority of the staff are not of northern European or North American heritage. In 2017–18, there were women (and one man) from multiple countries in Latin America—including Mexico, Ecuador, Brazil, and the Dominican Republic—and a team in Thailand. The doctor was Moldovan. There were three North Americans, one of whom had spent much of her adult life in Europe or Latin America. There was one person of Dutch ancestry working in the Amsterdam administrative office, but the other Europeans I spoke with had grown up in Poland under the communist system or in Portugal in the aftermath of decades of authoritarian government.

The relatively large number of Polish and Portuguese staff members is notable. On the one hand, it reflects the needs of the telemedicine help desk for speakers of those languages, with many email requests coming in from Poland and Brazil, as well as the history of Women on Waves campaigns in each country in the early 2000s. From a more geopolitical perspective, however, this means that the European perspectives within Women Help Women come largely from women who grew up within the extended Soviet-Communist system and the aftermath of its collapse, or in a country that was under authoritarian dictatorship until the mid-70s and then was forced to restructure its economy under IMF supervision in the early 2010s. The experience of Portugal in the late twentieth and early twenty-first century has more parallels to South America than to the dominant countries of western and northern Europe. Poland has also been through a series of sociopolitical transformations that have no parallel in western Europe, including a kind of de-secularization that has had profound gender implications. Part of the transnational flavor, and political perspective, of Women Help Women comes from the relative absence of those who grew up within the dominant cultures of the most economically powerful countries on the planet. I don't say this to idealize the politics or the internal dynamics of Women Help Women—just to point out that the sociopolitical location and perspective of an organization emerges from its members, and in this case, circa 2017–19, almost all came from globally nondominant backgrounds. The absence of African voices and perspectives among staff was notable, yet at the same time the European experiences represented within WHW could be described as a very different flavor of whiteness than in most Global North NGOs.

The intercontinental meetings and ongoing ties that have formed among frontline activists and organizations across the Global South offer another example of a transnational network, of a kind increasingly common in the world but not necessarily visible to many in North America. In 2016 and 2018, there were global meetings of hotline and accompaniment activists from Africa, Latin America, and Asia that were held in Indonesia, which at the time had a very well-organized and globally well-connected hotline (Samsara). The meetings were funded by northern donors, but attendees described them as an encounter with their peers from across the globe. As one activist from Ecuador put it,

> First of all it was really weird to travel to another continent, into the future . . . and see all these other women, I mean, the strategies you have in Asia, amazing, the strategies in Africa. So it was a learning experience, but also a chance to look at ourselves on the global level.

In the first meeting, in 2016, there were significant linguistic challenges around translation, and while this was handled much better in 2018, there continued to be issues around genuine cross-cultural understanding. From a Nigerian:

> I was like, "Wow, so we are among those people running the hotlines in the world" . . . They had translators, so they translated to English and Latin American Spanish . . . It was very difficult. Sometimes, it's hard to say something. It's hard to ask someone something [across the language divide].

An Argentinian activist expressed similar sentiments in different words:

> The first challenge is linguistic. You're in a gathering with people from Asia, from Africa, where you have to make an effort to translate not just words but meanings.

These linguistic and cultural challenges coexisted with a sense of great excitement over the diversity of representatives globally and from within each region; one of the outcomes of the 2016 meeting was actually the initiation of new regional network meetings within Africa and Latin America.

Activists who attended one or both of the international hotline meetings described them as a uniquely valuable location for expanding their understanding in both pragmatic and visionary ways. The Nigerian hotline manager emphasized the value of being in a place where she could share and compare experiences with others who were doing similar work, unlike at an international conference dominated by policy and research concerns:

> We get to know about how callers or how the hotline are being handled in other countries . . . You get a lot of experiences from other organizations . . . If you are having difficulties you have to present it there where you have a lot of colleagues, and you get answers from them. It's an opportunity to share.

These encounters among frontline activists from across the world brought more existential experiences as well; as one Argentinian put it:

> It makes me so proud to think we're a part of this movement, that we're busy creating, that we're imagining. And I often feel as if there are no limits to the imagination, and that's profoundly challenging . . . A movement is rapidly taking off all over the world, not only in Latin America but in Africa and Asia.

7

In It for the Long Term: The Lives of Committed Activists

How is it possible [to have a job]? I don't know. I do have a job that leaves me time to do this, I guess that's why I chose it. It's not the best-paid gig, it's with an NGO, and, in case you didn't know, in Ecuador the NGOs are the lowest of the low. But that allows me some freedom . . . I have to reach targets, and if I reach them, I'll see how I organize myself. I think it's to do with the way activists, especially in Latin America, which is what I know best, tend to have precarious jobs . . . And then of course some of us have three of them. And many of us aren't just responsible for ourselves, we have dependents, children, mothers. (Ecuador)

Television and movies often represent social movement participation as a brief moment in life, perhaps most stereotypically while someone is in college. Labor unions are the obvious exception to this, even at the level of media, but labor organizing in the United States is rarely shown in ways that look like a social movement—except perhaps for recent campaigns at Starbucks and Amazon, and even then the organizers profiled in the media were still young adults, even if they weren't students. Many people attend rallies when an event or issue feels important, and may have some broad identification with a movement, but are never committed activists; those who become committed activists for some period of time, however, are likely to move in and out of significant engagement with social movements throughout their lives.[1]

The activists who were part of this study have been committed feminists and SMA activists for many years, although some described stepping back from the movement for a time or shifting their roles. Direct action that takes place day after day, week after week, and year after year requires long-term commitment from a sizable core group of activists in order to be sustained and successful; this commitment is not a "hobby" or something to do on weekends but in practice comes to shape the contours of life at deep levels. The North American cultural ideology that work and family form the central commitments of adult lives and that everything else comes second (or should), erases or depoliticizes how people actually go about building their lives. When I was at the apartment of a Chilean activist that she shared with activist friends, there were pictures of her son around the living room, and she explained that he was currently with his dad in a shared custody arrangement. When her son was with her, he became part of a household of lesbian feminist activists and participated in whatever aspects of his mother's life seemed age and context appropriate—as with any other child who moves between parental households. Similarly, occupational and career decisions always involve some balance with life commitments, including to social movements, as in the quote above.

Research on the lives of social movement activists has found that long-term commitments and ongoing engagement with political work are common, not exceptional, and take a few different forms. First, it may be useful to note that studies of specific organizations or waves of social mobilization, such as Black Lives Matter, often come to the opposite conclusion: that participants engage for a relatively short period of time and then drop out. This may be true if you look at one specific organization or mobilization—but moving away from a particular organization or set of protests does not mean that someone ceases to be engaged as an activist. I have been a member of Jews for Racial and Economic Justice (JFREJ), a NYC-based organization, since 1995, but my level of active engagement has varied from committed volunteer organizer to co-chair of the board to long periods of being a dues-paying member who shows up to one or two events per year. During the same time period I have also been an active member of ACT UP NY, a member of an unauthorized syringe distribution collective, a member of a JFREJ offshoot called Jews Against the [Israeli] Occupation, a member of the Rise and Resist Actions Committee, and an on-call rally marshal for various iterations of dissident queer-identified alternative Pride marches. Mixed in with all that have been times in which I was not, in fact, an active and engaged member of any particular organization but went to events and was occasionally called on for support or training or advice of one kind or another by a *compañera/o*.

My trajectory is one example of long-term activism, moving in and out of periods of greater and lesser engagement depending on other demands on my life, but always living within communities formed around activist connections. My mother had a perhaps more common trajectory, as she was very engaged in leftist groups as a teenager and young adult in the 1940s and early '50s; then her activism shifted to periodic attendance at events during her marriage to my (nonactivist) father, although she was very politically engaged at work in different ways. After my father died, she threw herself back into social movement work of various kinds. Throughout her life, her closest friends were people she originally met through progressive organizing. When social movement commitment is measured by participation in one specific organization, then shifting one's energies to a different organization can look like dropping out of the movement—but research that follows the lives of activists, rather than organizations, generally finds sustained, if episodic, commitment.

Long-term, ongoing forms of direct action place different stresses and demands on both organizations and individuals than the use of brief, confrontational forms of action as one strategy within a larger campaign. Direct actions such as a rally or moving picket outside a targeted location or event generally require a meaningful amount of advance organizing, especially for an action that draws many people, but both the preparation and the action itself are focused and time limited. A civil disobedience action often requires more planning than a rally or picket, and the actual duration of the action lies in the hands of the police and the courts, but activists assess their own ability to participate in that particular moment. In contrast, the direct action of staffing a hotline or doing accompaniments intrinsically involves an ongoing, high-level commitment with a great deal of unpredictability. As described in chapter 3, a hotline has designated hours when the phones are answered, and individuals sign up for shifts, but within those hours it is impossible to know when or how often the phone will ring, what kind of attention any given call will require, or where the activist covering the shift will be when someone calls. Life doesn't stop just because you have the phone, and there are countless stories about answering it on the bus, during dinner, with your mother listening on the other side of a thin apartment wall, because you can't just say, "Sorry, I'm busy, can I call you back?" An accompaniment requires even more attention than a hotline, although with an accompaniment there are more possibilities for planning and for practical assistance from other activists. As an Ecuadorian activist says, "An accompaniment means being there, being present, the whole time, and so you plan your life to fit. That's why I say that we can work thanks to our networks." Social movement work generally takes up as much space as someone has available, plus a little more, but the movement for SMA shapes lives at deeper levels than many others given the nature of the work and social contexts surrounding it.

The structure of feminist support for SMA as a form of direct action may be unique in some ways, but as has been discussed throughout this book there are other movements that engage in related kinds of action. All movements depend on the knowledge and experience of long-term activists and make demands on participants that can disrupt daily life, but this is particularly true for movements focused on solidarity-based systems of support for people in marginalized, criminalized situations. These forms of direct action have to be continuous and long-term in order to be effective, and involve learning to be present with people who are not, typically, activists themselves and who are experiencing *involuntary* criminalization. I emphasize the word "involuntary" because activists may engage in actions that risk criminal penalties, such as carrying abortion pills across borders, but they do so as an intentional act in a political context; a person with an undesired pregnancy can be criminalized anywhere abortion is restricted or banned. In order to be effective, support must be reliable and the activists providing it need a minimum level of knowledge, both technically and interpersonally, in order to meet someone from a place of solidarity and care. This is as true of syringe exchange, for example, as of abortion accompaniment, and the direct-action strategies of both movements require predictable availability, considerable time, and a capacity for social/emotional presence with people managing stigmatized, criminalized situations with limited options. The dynamics of long-term commitment in this kind of work are complex and affect many areas of life more than engagement with other movements or forms of direct action.

This chapter will explore how and why people become active in the movement for SMA, and how a long-term commitment to this work comes to shape someone's life. The majority of people interviewed for this project had been involved in the movement for many years at the time of the interview, including people who had moved in and out or changed their roles over time. I'll look first at how different types of organizations shape their members' experience, and then go on to consider how activists first get involved and learn to manage some of the stresses and risks. Finally, I will explore how long-term involvement in feminist direct action for SMA shapes the lives and social worlds of activists.

Working at an NGO vs. Organizing in a Collective

The continuous and demanding nature of activist work can be challenging at organizational as well as individual levels, and the dynamics depend on the structure of the organization. As already discussed, the majority of SMA organizations in Latin America are collectives with a formally horizontal structure, while NGOs are the dominant form in Africa and among the international telehealth platforms. Mexico has some prominent NGOs, including the first organization to offer accompaniment, as well as many collectives. The United States appears to be developing in ways that are analogous to Mexico, with a cluster of highly visible NGOs and then a wide variety of networks and collectives, although the emerging US collectives and networks are currently less visible than those in Mexico given the intense politicization and rapidly evolving legal situation in the United States. The structure of an organization shapes activist experience in important ways, especially the contrast between a formal NGO and more informal activist collectives. Some of the information in this section may sound familiar from previous chapters, but in this chapter I am approaching it from a different perspective.

The processes of recruiting and training new members changes over time for collectives, and that shapes the experience of activist work. In chapter 3, I described how recruitment shifted from inner circles that required only basic orientation and technical training in medication abortion to a point where an Ecuadorian collective could put out a call for applicants to an abortion "school," where potential collective members would go through a process that combined technical training and political education, including discussions of values and goals. This recruitment shift from inner circles of friends to people who are completely new is not unique to Ecuador and presents multiple challenges for an unpaid collective—to both applicants and existing collective members alike. There's the obvious question of the time and effort required to run an extended recruitment and training program; even more, this type of recruiting creates a different internal culture than bringing in friends or friends of friends who already more or less share in the collective's existing values and ways of doing things. This shift away from inner-circle-focused recruitment and towards training and integration processes can have a significant effect on the dynamics of an informally structured horizontal collective. There may be cohort or generational differences in background, or issues with the potential power that trainers may have for some time in relation to trainees, as well as issues concerning the impact of new people on group culture.

Of course, changes in group culture are not necessarily a negative and in the long run may bring about new patterns that make the work more sustainable. An Ecuadorian describes an internal shift in the culture of a hotline collective:

> [Now,] we try to take care of our emotional security . . . [but when] I first started on the hotline, you had to toughen up, you got hard . . . A couple years ago some new women came into the group, and at one meeting they broke down . . . They started crying and saying to us: "You must be made of stone, of wood, you don't care."

Another member of the same collective agreed:

> We didn't used to have such a process of self-care . . . Now, I feel it can be a much more loving process . . . building these networks and strong mutual bonds that enable us to keep going.

These kinds of recruitment and training processes can look very different in NGOs where there are always some formal structures, some divisions of labor, and typically some vertical elements to decision-making. In my conversations with NGOs, the training and integration of new staff was talked about in relatively routine ways, and NGO workers commented on how training had increased and formalized since the early days of the organization when everyone was learning together and making it up as they went along. The management of power and hierarchy within feminist NGOs (and collectives) is its own separate branch of feminist literature, and I have no interest in delving into those issues within specific organizations. For the purposes of this book, and this chapter, the important point is that the formal structures of the NGO world offer different frameworks and create different organizational cultures than the informal structures of collectives—and, of course, NGOs pay their staff. All these things deeply shape the experiences of activists and affect how (or sometimes if) they make a long-term commitment to the work.

Some of the NGOs that I met with were deeply involved in creating systems that were as horizontal and open as possible, while others expressed less concern about decision-making structures, at least in conversations with me. In either case, however, it's quite different to hire and train new staff than it is to integrate new (volunteer) members into a horizontal collective; the technical, medical, and feminist values clarification materials were relatively similar for both NGOs and autonomous groups, but the organizational dynamics surrounding the process seemed more fraught in the collectives than the NGOs.

These different dynamics of formal and informal structures play out in relation to security practices as well. As discussed in chapter 4, digital security is a central concern for all the groups I had contact with, and most were consciously integrating a holistic approach that emphasized the social and psychological as well as the digital and legal. All the organizations described security as both challenging and necessary for safety and to maintain operations over the long term. Again, the formal systems of employment at an NGO created an organizational environment in which a certain amount of standardization around security practices was relatively straightforward. The NGOs held sessions and meetings on security practices that were part of an ordinary workday, in contrast to the security training for a collective, which was an addition to regular activist meetings, and of course in addition to one's separate, paid workday. The issue of what one is paid to do and what is done on one's "own time" is profound although rarely directly mentioned by members of collectives. The tensions surrounding differential commitment could be directly addressed at times, as they were here by one Ecuadorian activist:

> Trouble begins when there's no uniform preparation across the network. If some compañeras are a little less committed than others, that causes a security vacuum. I mean that for me, it's really important that we're all on the same page . . . because security is what allows us to function as a network, what enables us to sustain ourselves, what makes it possible for us to accompany women.

On the question of vulnerability to the extreme right and evangelical activists, the relative organizational position of collectives versus NGOs reverses and the informality of collectives becomes a significant strength. None of the Latin American collectives expressed concern about the impact of evangelical activists on their safety and operations in an ongoing way. Some talked about the ways increased politicization of abortion and the growth of far-right evangelical churches affected their engagement with political action in public space, as when the July 25 march in Santiago was attacked or when an Ecuadorian activist described "thinking twice" about taking part in direct actions. Harassing callers who try to get hotline workers to break the law have been a constant feature of work on the hotlines, but these are perceived as an annoyance more than a threat.

In contrast, the NGOs in Africa and in Mexico City all engaged in some form of self-protection in relation to far-right actors, and two took steps to obscure their locations (as described in chapter 4). The address for one Mexican NGO doesn't appear on Google: it just says "unnamed road, Zona Central Comercial" and the city. By definition, an NGO has a formal address (even if it doesn't appear on Google) and is registered with the state, which makes them more literally "locatable" than a collective. In addition, NGOs generally interact with traditional media, and will issue statements and participate in media programs of various kinds, all of which exposes them (and their individual staff) to a wider array of potential attacks. These forms of visibility are simultaneously essential for the long-term success of NGOs, including their fundraising profile, yet generate a certain level of risk in relation to harassment and threats. A collective exists in a more diffuse way and can choose those forms of visibility that feel politically efficacious (Facebook pages, wheat-pasted flyers) while downplaying those that create unnecessary risk, like a public street address or appearances on talk shows.

The differences between NGOs and collectives shape individual experiences as well as organizational processes, and will thread through each section below as I explore how involvement in the movement for SMA has shaped the lives of activists, from their initial contact through the time of the interview.

Becoming an Abortion Activist

Many feminists in the United States are currently asking themselves how one gets involved in the movement for SMA, for very pragmatic political reasons. The stories that I heard about how and why women got involved all reflected a desire to do something practical and immediately useful for women facing a potentially life-altering situation, a concern that is also very alive in the United States today. In the United States, there seems to be a cultural inclination to see personal experience as the driving force behind public action, as when survivors of rape or gun violence become anti-violence activists—but among the SMA activists I spoke with, only two people told personal stories related to abortion. One woman described helping a friend get an abortion in Ecuador when she was seventeen; she was from a middle-class family and was able to find a feminist gynecologist to help them. The other story was from one of the few older women to participate, who talked about her experience as a single mother with a son (who was a wanted child) and understanding how it might feel to be a woman who finds herself pregnant in a state where abortion is banned and unmarried pregnancy highly stigmatized. For the majority of people I interviewed, involvement with SMA grew out of engagement with other political organizing or community work, although there were some differences regionally as well as between collectives and NGOs.

At the most general level, many of the activists I spoke with became involved with the movement for SMA during a transitional period in their lives when making a significant commitment to something new was relatively easy. Universities, of course, provide an almost stereotypical pathway into political engagement and activism, and this may be especially true in Latin America. Almost all of the Latin American activists talked about becoming involved in progressive student movements while in university, initially in leftist movements and then with feminist groups. These groups often had a strong theoretical/intellectual orientation, and the direct action of a hotline offered a sharp contrast to activism centered on debate across theoretical and analytical positions. The desire for more practical direct action was especially true for women from more working-class backgrounds, but the focus on concrete action was important to everyone who became involved in SMA. It is important to note, however, that while many long-term, committed activists first became involved as students, the movement for SMA has never been a student movement. As described in previous chapters, the Ecuadorian hotline was created by a feminist NGO led by young adults, and the Concepción branch of the Chilean hotline emerged from a long-standing feminist group in the city. The activists who joined collectives as students then carried this commitment forward into their post-university life, as in the experience of this Ecuadorian woman:

> I was a student, maintained by my parents—I lived with them, so my lodging, food, and transport were all paid for by them and I had more free time. So the pattern was: study, homework, go out with friends, and, on certain days, answer the hotline phone . . . After that I graduated from college and got a job. Since then, I work an eight-hour day; when it's my turn for phone duty, I go over there to do it; the line is open from five p.m. to ten.

In Africa, the relationship between education and involvement in SMA work takes a very different form. Many of the women who came to work for the NGOs in Nigeria and Kenya were initially drawn in through workshops on sexual and reproductive health or women's rights, and many had already been engaged and visible in their communities as organizers of some kind, as this Kenyan woman describes:

> In the community, I work as a CBT, community-based trainer, training women about leadership, finance, banking. Then I thought of going beyond whatever I'm doing. I decided to look into reproductive health. That's when I came and joined [the Kenyan NGO].

Prior involvement in some kind of organizing is particularly common for activists in Kenya, where the hotline was created by an organization already doing health- and rights-related work within low-income communities:

> How I met [the Kenyan NGO] is they wanted to work with girls in Korogocho . . . I started being engaged in some of their activities . . . After that, we've also worked in some radio information and educating the girls about contraceptives, abortion, which [was] not legal in Kenya . . . That was like ten years ago. So, I've been really involved in a lot of things.

The Nigerian organization was founded by a teacher and women's rights activist, and the staff includes some of her former students as well as women who first came to an event and returned later as staff. One Nigerian activist described her introduction to the NGO this way: "When I finished my secondary school, I wasn't doing anything. So, [my former teacher] called me. I heard about the program they are going to do." Another former student was supported through a training program before being hired:

> Throughout my stay in that school for learning computer operation, they paid for it. After the program, she now said, okay, I can come in and work for her. I said okay, no problem. You've helped me to acquire knowledge knowing how to operate a computer. I would like to be a part of this organization.

Though the directors of each NGO had significant ties to feminist movements nationally and transnationally, this was largely not true of the regular staff before being hired. This is a distinct difference between the two African NGOs and the other organizations, including NGOs in other countries, where people came to the NGO or collective as engaged feminists seeking a new avenue for their activism.

The staff of Women Help Women (WHW), the international telemedicine platform, have some distinct patterns for involvement linked to the international character of the organization and its close ties with grassroots collectives and NGOs around the world. Given the central role of WHW and its founding staff within the movement transnationally, continuing into the present, it's worthwhile to understand how people come to work for the organization. As in Latin America, all of the staff I spoke with were politically engaged and feminist identified before starting to work on SMA—and the Latin American staff at WHW have histories similar to other SMA activists from the region. In fact, many worked with local collectives and were later hired by the telemedicine platform, sometimes while continuing earlier work with a collective. Overall, there are (or were) three general pathways through which staff come to work for the telemedicine platform.

One pathway to WHW, referenced above, is that activists are hired out of grassroots groups, often as a result of shared work of some kind. One Portuguese activist who came to work for WHW was directly involved with the Portugal side of a Women on Waves visit, as discussed in chapter 1, and others in Portugal were directly or indirectly drawn to working with the platform as a result of the Waves visit and the overall struggle to legalize abortion in Portugal. Similarly, the Polish activists were drawn to Women on Waves, and later WHW, based on the organization's work in Poland and the ongoing need for support with SMA there. A Thai activist with a long history of HIV work was part of a collective operating a Thai abortion website; she described being trained on SMA in an afternoon so that she could start answering telemedicine emails for WHW from Thailand. One of the founders of the Ecuadorian hotline was hired in the early 2010s, and a Venezuelan hotline activist was hired after she moved to France.

A second pathway to WHW results from the location of the administrative offices in Amsterdam, a distinctly international city that draws people from around the world who often arrive during a somewhat unstable or transitional time in their lives. When I visited Amsterdam in 2017 only one of the office staff was of Dutch heritage, and I don't think that number has increased much since. A few of the staff arrived first for internships and are all now regular employees although only one remained in Amsterdam. In the early 2000s, two relatively young Polish women arrived in the city, one on her own and the other married to a Dutchman, and both were drawn to Women on Web in part because they knew about the Waves boat campaign in Poland—and later were key to the creation of WHW. A Mexican woman came with her husband, whose job took him to Amsterdam, and she began to volunteer at Women on Web, then was hired and worked part-time after she went back to Mexico. These former Web employees went on to be part of WHW. While some come to the city and remain, the online nature of the work means that people who come as interns or for some other temporary reason can continue to work for the organization regardless of where they go.

Finally, there are some professionals who were already committed feminist activists within their field and were drawn to the work of the organization. For example, the doctor who works with WHW is an international expert and advocate connected to several international medical groups focused on abortion, in addition to being licensed in a country with liberal prescribing laws in relation to medication abortion. There are several lawyers across the Americas who work on advocacy and legal issues related to SMA under the larger umbrella of WHW, although they are all primarily employed at a university or progressive legal institute of some kind. An American feminist who has long been involved in reproductive justice in the United States began to work with Women on Waves in the early to mid-2000s, and has become very involved in the emergence of SMA both internationally and in the United States, largely through her work with WHW. These professionals who come to work in SMA are not exactly the same as a group whom I will describe later in this chapter as "SMA professionals"; professionals who do some work in SMA are not intrinsically visible as activists, while the group I call "SMA professionals" come to be extremely visible as activists in the field in a way that shapes their lives outside of work.

At the beginning of this section, I said that many activists first become involved in the movement for SMA during a transitional period in their lives. Whether these activists were politicized as university students, hired by NGOs, or came to Amsterdam for an internship, a time of transition could open up for them significant new pathways. The US Supreme Court overturned *Roe* as I wrote this book, and there are committed activists in the United States who are now trying to figure out how to integrate direct action for SMA into their lives. I find myself wondering whether a significant political change, combined with the social instabilities and changes from the COVID pandemic, will create some of the openness to new commitments that can be seen in the more ordinary life cycle changes described here. There has been an explosion of interest in SMA, but at the end of the fall of 2022 it is still too early to know what form a wave of new SMA activists and organizations within the United States may take.

Who Gets to Know What You Do?

The stigma around abortion, and its politicization and criminalization, has transformed a fairly common event in women's lives into a loaded topic for ordinary conversation. The majority of activists I spoke with engaged in some level of information control in regard to their work around SMA, especially when they first got involved. Some tightly controlled who knew about their activism as a matter of security, to avoid problems at work, or to maintain familial relationships, while others developed strategies for answering ordinary questions without mentioning the word "abortion" to avoid annoying conversations. For example, a woman who lives in France and works for a telemedicine platform described the situation this way:

> When you say that you work in abortion . . . you start this conversation. So, here in France, if I don't say anything it's because sometimes you get tired of—it's like for doctors when they say that they are doctors, "Oh my feet hurt."

And, of course, for others it's just one of the obvious, well-known facts of their lives—as a Chilean woman told me, "*soy feminista, lesbiana, abortista,*" "I am a feminist, a lesbian, an abortionist"—but her casual summary doesn't mean that these identities have not presented problems in her life. We all limit information at times to protect privacy and avoid undesired social interactions, and some of what was described to me falls into that zone, but overall there was a significant level of attention to the boundaries around who knows, who doesn't, and how that changes over time.

The activists I spoke with were not new to the movement for SMA and had created familiar, if not always completely comfortable, patterns of information flow in their personal lives. Communication with family was often mixed by some combination of gender and generation, with sisters the most likely to know about someone's abortion activism and older relatives the least likely to know. From Chile:

> I haven't told my family that I'm involved in accompaniment. Family, as in parents and siblings. I've told my nieces, though . . . if you or a friend need an abortion, let me know.

She went on to describe the boundaries she keeps outside the family, using the formal pronoun *usted* to signify that "the rest" with whom she shares information anonymously are not friends or family:

> I only tell my girlfriends that I'm in this process of accompaniment. To the rest I merely provide information, like someone who happens to know. "Ah, if you need it, here, here's the email of [Chilean accompaniment]."

Some were completely open with family members, though this may have taken time. An Ecuadorian woman who lived with her mother when she first began to work with the hotline told me,

> I went through a process of opening up to my family and at the same time of self-acceptance . . . empowering myself, coming out of the closet and saying, "Yes, I'm a feminist and I'm proabortion."

As is often true in adult life, a personal circle of friends knows more about the details of your day-to-day life than family members, and this may be especially true of political activists, as for this Ecuadorian woman:

> When you become an activist, a lot of things change for you . . . My compañeras are also my closest friends, with whom I've gone through so many moments and spaces of life.

It's also worth acknowledging that keeping information from parents and family can create tensions that are not based in social or political disagreement, as in these reflections from another Ecuadorian activist:

> Looking back, today, over about eleven years . . . I feel in a way it cost me my career, because we were often hard at it for fifteen,

> twenty hours, because everything was urgent. And I remember how it caused a bunch of trouble with my family. They'd go, "You've got to study, you've got to prioritize that," and I'd go, "No, this is our moment, we're in the middle of something great."

On the other hand, she was talking about being part of the original hotline collective in Ecuador, so she was right—they were creating something big that was the start of an important movement.

Information control in one's personal life can be easier for those who work for NGOs, since the phone doesn't ring at home in the evening, and you can always just say that you work for a women's health organization. From an activist in Nigeria:

> They don't know that I work with the hotline . . . I talk to them basically on a social worker level . . . I have this information. I work with an organization that is with sexual reproductive health rights. I get information from them. I pass it to them. And then I tell them there is a hotline you can reach, so whatever information that they need, they call the hotline.

For NGO staff, the desire to manage disclosure can have many motivations but often revolves around the consequences of stigma and social discomfort. Similar to the activist in France, a Portuguese woman working for the telemedicine platform also described the challenges of raising the issue of abortion, even in a country where it is legal:

> For a long time, I didn't talk to many people about my work, because I didn't want to bother them with it because it's an uncomfortable topic . . . I'm not the type of person so interested in arguments . . . In a sense, the work is also difficult because it's not a fun topic.

The African activists described having to actively negotiate the question of religion as they thought about what information to share in their personal lives, but this did not always mean they kept quiet about their work. One Nigerian woman decided not to argue with her mother:

> My mom is a very religious type . . . She wouldn't understand [my work] at all, based on her own religious beliefs . . . I don't sit down with her and make an argument on [abortion] because she won't buy it. But that's the truth. She will not buy it because she is positioned where she's positioned, and that is who she is.

However, another Nigerian activist periodically makes the issue of abortion visible within her own church community:

> I'm a soloist in the church. So, most of my choir members, when they see [an abortion post on Facebook], and be like, "Oh, so on Sunday, after posting this information, you come back to the church and sing"[imitating an accusing tone] . . . But after everything you see some of them coming to you indirectly. You know, "Please, that thing that you posted, how does it work? I don't know my—I have a problem."

Support for SMA may create challenges in relation to one's job or career, but it can also be a job or a career for those in NGOs and abortion-related professions. Within the world of NGOs, those who work at lower and mid-levels answering hotlines and telemedicine emails, running workshops of various kinds, and working in coordination or middle management roles, have significant latitude to decide how open they want to be about work in their personal lives, as reflected in the quotes above. Those who represent an organization to the public in media of various kinds or in any other public context have an entirely different experience; it is their job to be a public face of SMA. This can have minor, humorous elements, as when someone commented that she couldn't carry pills in her luggage when she travels "because no one would believe it was for my dog," but can also be far more serious. In chapter 4, I described a Mexican activist who was under significant threat from the far right after she appeared on a television program. At a less serious level, an activist from Poland who lives in Amsterdam said she finally did the paperwork to get a Dutch passport after appearing on the cover of a Polish women's magazine. A television interview or a photo for a magazine are completely ordinary and expected aspects of work for senior NGO management, but can have unanticipated consequences for someone working in abortion.

The balance between activism and work requires significant attention for members of collectives, for whom the (paid) workplace can be at least as complex an environment to negotiate as their families. A lawyer who is part of a local accompaniment collective and also does movement legal work, including for one of the telemedicine platforms, makes a careful distinction between what is shareable and what isn't:

> The matter of accompaniment, I do keep it as—well, for the sake of everyone's security and that of the organization, I don't mention accompaniment as such . . . but I do say that I work with abortion and with [WHW].

Likewise, a junior professor at a Chilean university said that some of her colleagues knew what she did, but that once she began to say too much in the presence of a senior colleague and had to cut things off by describing herself as a "militant feminist"—knowing that would end the conversation since "you can't ask what that means."

For highly educated Chilean activists, the government in the 2010s was a complicated source of employment that brought both risk and opportunity, and the women's division presented the most problems given the political controversy surrounding abortion:

> I worked in a government office for three years. It wasn't advisable for me to be directly associated with self-managed abortion, not because I was ashamed but because I'd be fired. I was pretty discreet with all that, given that there were people at work who knew I belonged to a feminist collective, that I'd been involved in abortion, that I was with the hotline; but they were good accomplices . . . They never said a thing about it.

Other activists worked for progressive NGOs that were not necessarily abortion related, or had jobs that had no relation to politics at all. In Ecuador, one woman managed a travel agency and another worked for a library, both positions that allowed scheduling flexibility when needed and where their politics were known, respected by at least some coworkers, and generally irrelevant to the job. The relationship between work and activism for those in collectives will be picked up again in the next section of this chapter on how activism gives shape to a life.

In the most repressive countries, like Brazil and Poland, the issue of information control in one's personal life was inseparable from concerns about holistic security more than about familial relationships, although the two overlap as regards the psychological and emotional elements of security. This is part of the challenge confronting activists in the United States where, like in Poland and Brazil, abortion has become highly politicized and rights for women in general have been attacked. Two activists in Brazil described their experiences with living and working in an extremely repressive environment, and how security concerns become woven into day-to-day communication. The first focused on some of the realities of information management for people across different social movements under Bolsonaro:

> People have cover stories. People don't say where they go when they have to travel for meetings or things like that. And these add some stress because—entering into this dynamic where you have to lie all the time, you have to come up with stories all the time, and then you have to make sure that you will remember that story when people ask.

The second described her experience in relation to friends and family, and how holistic security practices have improved support among movement activists:

> My sister, she's the only one that knows . . . My previous friends, before I got involved—they don't know, and my family doesn't know . . . The persecution of the social movement [for abortion] is crazy, and it's getting worse—so my sister gets worried about that. But I just tell her, "No, I'm doing everything—don't worry. I have lawyers," and then she's just, "Okay, go. I trust you—you go for it" . . . In the past two, three years, there has been growth in the culture of digital security for feminists. And this has been helping a lot to break this isolation, because people have now a little bit of knowledge on how to get in touch, how to communicate and not feel unsafe.

Giving Shape to One's Life

In the quote that opens the chapter, an Ecuadorian woman says that many activists have three jobs—their activism, their paid employment, and caring for their family. Feminists in the United States have long talked about the second shift that women manage in relation to work and family, and how those two interact. The level of attention required to answer a hotline or accompany an abortion *cuando me toca*—"when it's my turn" but more literally "when it touches me"—is more than an additional task to be handled during a busy month. Rather, it is work that comes to shape the contours of a life. When I asked the Ecuadorian activist how it was possible to have a job, she said, "I don't know." But in reality, everyone I met in the collectives of Latin America found ways to work, have children if they wanted, and stay connected to the movement in evolving ways.

The creation of social and friendship networks is one of the central ways that activism shapes people's lives, and one of the ways that activists manage the stresses and challenges of being immersed in work around SMA. This is especially true for members of collectives, who often live within social worlds largely created through their movement networks, both within and beyond SMA. An activist from Ecuador:

> I've been active in social and feminist movements ever since I was seventeen; I guess I've spent most of my life as a militant. My son grew up in that environment, he's pals with the other kids in there . . . My compañeras are also my closest friends, with whom I've gone through so many moments and spaces of life.

Activist compañeras can also make it possible for people to remain connected to the movement during periods of increased familial demand, perhaps especially within accompaniment collectives, as was this woman's experience when her son was very young:

> [I said] I can't, it's too much for me, for my life . . . They allowed me greater flexibility and to adjust the time I spend. With an accompaniment, you don't measure the time.

In Chile, which had extremely repressive laws when I was in and out of Santiago in 2017 and 2018, there were at least three feminist households that I knew of where women who knew each other through movement networks also lived together as roommates. These households and friendship networks create a world within which information control is less of an issue, and where the kinds of commitments and security concerns involved are taken for granted. As one of the Brazilians said, "I think that the long-term activists, they have very diverse friends. But they are all activists even if from different areas."

The issues of time, boundaries, personal life, and work with hotlines or accompaniment can be especially salient in relation to partners on evenings and weekends. There were plenty of comments, mostly outside of interviews, around the conundrum of whether to date within or outside of the movement, the benefits and costs (for collectives as well as individuals) of each strategy. For some it is not actually a question: "To have a partner who's not an activist . . . personally I could never, we wouldn't have anything to talk about."

Activists with children balance multiple definitions of a good partner:

> It's quite difficult with my partner because we can't sort of talk in depth, he questions my housework, my job, my feminism . . . At the same time he's a very hands-on dad, and there are other nice things about him, but in terms of me as a person and my own journey, it's more complicated, there are a few misunderstandings.

Others described partners who were relaxed about it: "'Sweetheart, we won't be talking today, I'm on hotline duty,' and he just gets on with his own stuff, he knows I need space and time for myself." And some had partners who were completely supportive: "He supports me in the collective, at college, in everything. He's a rock." But even with supportive partners, in this case lesbian, a hotline can sometimes be experienced as an intrusion on shared life: "I've got a partner, and it can be very awkward when I'm doing the hotline and we're together or whatever."

The issue of jobs and careers, whether inside or outside the movement, is one of the central ways in which activism shapes life. Those in collectives need jobs that do not conflict with commitments to activism and offer a combination of political openness (or indifference) and schedule flexibility. The combination is easier in the NGO sector than many others, and perhaps most difficult for professionals who cannot openly combine their activist and professional work in some way. The experience of professionals appears to reflect the larger political environment; for example, there is visible overlap between academia (at all levels) and the Socorristas in Argentina, while in Chile (more restrictive both legally and culturally) the SMA activists with academic jobs were relatively quiet about what they did on their own time. There is a clear distinction here between work on abortion as a policy or public health issue and the direct actions associated with SMA, with the former far more respectable than the latter, as in the comments earlier from a law professor who was open about her legal work with Women Help Women but not about her participation in a local collective. As one of the Ecuadorians said, reflecting on her own experience and that of others she knows, "I think it's to do with the way activists, especially in Latin America, which is what I know best, tend to have precarious jobs." Her association of precarious work with Latin American activists reflects the near universality of collectives across the region, in contrast to places where hotlines within NGOs can be a paid gig.

In contrast to the world of collectives, within an NGO the work of directly supporting women with SMA may lie at the heart of the organization but can, for most, be treated as something closer to a job with work/life boundaries. There are shifts that need to be filled, whether answering a hotline in an African call center or emails for a telemedicine service, and when a shift is over someone else picks up the work or, after hours, messages accumulate to be answered in the morning. In contrast, the highly visible NGO roles that I described earlier as "SMA professionals" may erode the boundaries between "work life" and "personal life," as these professionals become public faces for SMA. NGO administration is a notoriously boundaryless form of work in any field, but in regard to abortion in general and SMA in particular the question of visibility functions differently than ordinary problems with administrative workload. SMA professionals who interact with mass media in any way effectively lose some level of control over information disclosure, although the ways in which that shapes their lives depends on context: in Amsterdam, for example, it might expose you to undesired arguments but create some risk of official harassment when crossing the border into Poland.

Above all, though, activism shapes life in ways that have nothing to do with security and logistics. Activists in Africa talked about the impact of SMA work on their lives from a more personal and self-reflective perspective than activists elsewhere, though they articulated experiences that were implicit in many of the other interviews. A young Nigerian woman described a deep change in her sense of confidence:

> [This work] has really changed my life . . . Before, I can't talk to people. I can't. But now I—no matter the amount of women or whoever, I stand, and I talk because I am proud of what I'm talking about. And I'm happy that I have enough information to pass on to those women that really need it. So, it has really changed my life.

African activists also talked about how this work transformed their relationships despite strong social pressure surrounding traditional gender roles and religion:

> [This work] has a very deep impact. In fact, it set me up for life. Because for the first time—I never knew that a woman, you could decide when to marry. All I knew is that most times, they will bring in a suitor for you, and even as a young graduate, they started coming . . . But after the series of training, I just thought that this is my life and I need to do something.

The same activist went on to say,

> I happen to be a vice president of a church. A youth organization for over four years . . . I met people that are pregnant, and they will come for—I don't know if it's for prayers or for anything. But what I will ask them first is, "Do you actually want to keep it?"

A Kenyan community worker in a Muslim area reflected on the profound changes in her community and her role within it,

> When I began, it really had a negative impact . . . Through my passion, I decided this cannot limit me. So, I just have that courage through friends, through the network that I have, and the trainings which give me courage, then I started going down to the ground, talking to women, then after talking to the communities, they started giving the support.

The experience of taking action with others in order to change your world in some way has transformative elements for anyone who becomes deeply involved in activist work, and this is probably the most powerful way that it shapes your life. This can be particularly true when that action simultaneously changes your own location in your community.

Many women described shifts in their organizational roles or levels of engagement in SMA work over time, but movement connections and commitments continue to shape their lives. For example, most of the Latin American accompaniment activists I spoke with first became involved with hotlines in the early years of the movement, from 2008 to around 2011, and either helped found or joined accompaniment groups. This reflects the history of the movement and the emergence of accompaniment as a central strategy across the region during the mid-2010s, not a pattern of involvement that starts with one form of action and then shifts to another. Most importantly, most of the women I interviewed in Latin America became involved in the early years of the movement and still remained involved ten years later. Within NGOs, people shift roles over time, sometimes taking on more responsibility—such as a coordinator role—and sometimes stepping back to "just answer emails" (aka take a break) for a while.

In the last few years, I know that three of the women I interviewed left the organizations they had been involved with, but only one seems to have stepped back from activism, immigrating to the United States with a partner in search of new socioeconomic opportunities. Many lifelong activists have periods of their lives when they become less engaged with political organizing only to return to it at some later time, so I make no assumptions about what her trajectory will be over time. Of the other two, one was part of a collective that shifted their work from a local hotline to an online lesbian-feminist radio station; the other finished her PhD and is now connected to feminism and SMA primarily in a research context.

It is difficult to say much about the United States in regard to long-term participation since the movement for SMA is relatively new here. At the moment, it seems to mostly involve NGOs with an online presence, and networks built around existing forms of community activism. There are websites like Plan C and Reproaction that have existed for several years and were created by committed feminists, women whose activism has clearly shaped their lives and careers in many ways. The founders of Plan C, for example, have paid some professional price in their research careers for the visibility of their work with Plan C—and if anything, that seems to have inspired greater visibility from them as a response, not less.

Being part of the movement for SMA has been a profound experience for the people I interviewed, not only when they first got involved but in an ongoing way. The Ecuadorian woman who described telling her parents to leave her alone, that she and her friends were doing something important, turned out to be absolutely right, and she never expressed any regrets about the commitments she made as a young woman who was part of creating something that became the start of a movement. This kind of activist work shapes people's lives at deep levels through the transformative experience of direct action that changes their understanding of what is possible, not as individual achievement or a singular moment of victory but as ongoing shared work. This experience of transformation and long-term commitment was also true of needle exchange, especially in the early years, and other forms of solidarity-based direct action. The stories of SMA activists and others involved in similar movements show that collective action in solidarity with people in marginal, criminalized locations can change your understanding of self, community, and what is possible in the world.

Conclusion: Moving Forward

For many of the sectors who rule this world, we're committing an offense. And so, on this sometimes slippery ledge we're moving along, I think we're also developing a kind of feminism that's prepared to face the risks involved in doing these accompaniments. (Argentina)

The summer and fall of 2022 is an interesting moment to be writing about abortion in general and SMA in particular, with different pathways opening up in all directions. Globally, the COVID-19 pandemic dramatically raised the visibility of medication abortion and SMA as medical services reduced in-person care, telemedicine became the primary form of nonemergency care in many developed countries, and people still needed abortions. In places where abortion has long been tightly restricted, especially Latin America, social and legal change has opened up new possibilities and opportunities for feminists and people who can become pregnant. In other parts of the world, rights long taken for granted have come under threat and in some cases, most prominently in the United States, have been reversed. An increasingly global right wing uses gender and sexuality as accessible points of entry into movements that promote "traditional values" based in minimally concealed White supremacy. The visible pathways forward travel through dangerous territory but also hold the possibility of the deep changes that will take us to a future built on justice—a future built on a stronger foundation than the one the United States has lost.

Across Latin America, access to legal abortion has expanded significantly in the last few years. First Argentina legalized abortion through 14 weeks in December of 2020, then in 2021, a few weeks after Texas banned abortion after six weeks of pregnancy, the Mexican Supreme Court ruled that it is unconstitutional to regulate abortion through criminal law. In Feb 2022, the Colombian courts legalized abortion without restrictions through twenty-four weeks. All of these rulings include SMA since they are framed broadly, unlike the *Roe* decision in the United States that legalized abortion through a decision based on privacy and medical care. The inclusion of SMA is not something to take for granted, since legalization within the medical system does not intrinsically include abortion without medical supervision. Legal access to abortion is still tightly restricted in Chile, but the stigma and criminalization have both decreased. Moving north and across the Atlantic, another Catholic former colony, the Republic of Ireland, passed a constitutional amendment (66 percent in favor) in 2018 that enabled the legalization of abortion, and a law quickly enacted this through twelve weeks without restrictions.

In other parts of the Global North, however, the erosion of democracy by right-wing movements has been associated with the loss of reproductive rights and bodily autonomy for women and marginalized sexuality and gender populations. Poland has increasingly restricted access to abortion since the 1990s, after the fall of Communism, and now virtually all abortions are banned even if some formal access remains; women largely travel to Germany, Holland, or other European countries, or self-manage their abortions. In Hungary, abortion is technically legal but in practice there are so many barriers to access within the medical system that many women find it easier to go to Germany or

Austria. Russia and Central Europe have become centers for global far-right organizing that mobilize gender and sexuality as the entry point to a comprehensive ultra-conservative policy platform. The politics of abortion in Poland have received significant attention in recent years, but it is important to place that as a key dynamic within an overarching politic of gender, sexuality, and the erosion of democracy that is not limited to Poland.

In the United States, the politics of gender and sexuality also provide a visible surface or leading edge for a larger antidemocratic and White supremacist authoritarianism. The *Dobbs* decision reflects the outcome of systematic right-wing organizing over decades in which anxieties about race, gender, and sexuality are intermixed to support and enable the steady erosion of democratic institutions. The sweep of antiabortion court decisions and legislation goes against majority opinion nationally, as do the threats to LGBTQ+ rights that have reemerged simultaneously in many of the same states. This legislative combination demonstrates the power of prior antidemocratic processes, from the endless proliferation of restrictions on voting through the structure of the Senate and the Electoral College. However, the power of progressive values and voting is also visible, even in Republican states, as demonstrated in 2022 by the resounding defeat of antiabortion amendments to state constitutions in Kansas and Kentucky and the overall rejection of candidates who overtly questioned the 2020 elections.

The emergence of SMA in the United States follows a very different trajectory than across the Global South, where the movement initially emerged outside the medical system. In Latin America and Africa, SMA provided an alternative to dangerous and/or unreliable procedures in a context of, at best, highly restricted legal access. In the contexts where the first hotlines and accompaniment groups were created, abortion was restricted or banned but not necessarily highly politicized, which allowed some space within which organizations could experiment and develop coherent legal frameworks as well as solidarity and support strategies. The pathway from legal to illegal, traveled in very different ways by Poland and the United States, is intrinsically and profoundly politicized, which dramatically changes the risk environment for SMA. In the months immediately following the *Dobbs* decision, medication abortion occupied center stage as both a solution to state-level bans and a focus of right-wing attention. Everyone seems to agree that access to medication will be a key element of resistance and target of enforcement.

This terrain locates SMA as a political football used by all sides of the struggle, which amplifies the risks for activists as well as people seeking abortions in states with restrictive laws. In countries where abortion has long been restricted, the emergence of SMA may resolve some problems for local health authorities by reducing the destructive health consequences of abortion outside the medical system. However, when something carries significant political capital for both the left and the right, then official actors lose the option to quietly pay no attention, since someone will notice. As abortion bans spread through southern and midwestern states, conservative politicians and think tanks are already working to develop legal language to explicitly criminalize all forms of support and assistance for abortion, including or even especially for SMA. Whatever happens within the courts, and the culture, these attempts to prohibit solidarity and support for abortion demonstrate the intention to aggressively enforce abortion law and the perception that this carries significant political benefit.

The Ecuadorian hotline emerged in a context of broad progressive mobilization and cross-movement alliances that made activists feel protected, and it will be vital to remember that progressive solidarity carries power even in the current US context of right-wing mobilization. In the days after the *Dobbs* decision, LGBTQ+ Pride marches in cities across the United States demonstrated a clear understanding of the interconnections among different forms of bodily autonomy, with protests in support of abortion as well as trans and queer rights. The massive mobilizations of Black Lives Matter two years earlier, after the murder of George Floyd, created and solidified networks of experienced activists who emerged from a movement with a strong Black feminist and queer perspective and an intersectional analysis of power. There have been a series of successful, progressive union-organizing drives against previously untouchable corporations like Amazon and Starbucks. An increasingly militant climate justice movement has emerged over the past few years, often led by young adults who understand clearly that their lives depend on creating profound change. The fight for voting rights has become prominent once again, with some significant victories brought about by grassroots mobilizations from the left of the Democratic Party. It would be dangerously paralyzing to only look at the right wing and discount progressive mobilizations; reversing the current situation in the United States will require expansive solidarity and a clear antiracist and feminist human rights agenda, not incremental legal compromise.

The movement for SMA has been transformative globally, from the lives of activists to the lives of people who need abortions to public health statistics and research. As the United States moves deeper into the world created by the *Dobbs* decision, existing communities of solidarity are adapting and expanding their work and new ones are forming. Some networks of doulas and midwives in the United States have quietly added support for abortion into their repertoire of care for pregnant people, and abortion funds have integrated information about SMA into their health education portfolios, all of which began long before COVID or the fall of *Roe* but has increased in the last year. A sex worker organization that does outreach and advocacy is building a relationship with SMA activists in Mexico. A few syringe exchange programs in the southern United States are learning more about SMA, and figuring out how they can integrate information and referrals into the list of ways they can help their participants. A safe abortion should be an ordinary reality, and the power of this movement has been to create this reality—or at least the potential for it—outside the control of laws and medical institutions through building communities of solidarity.

This book explored strategies used around the world, particularly in the Global South, to facilitate access to abortion through support for SMA in contexts of restricted access. I think the question for those of us in the United States over the coming months and years will be, "How can we develop solidarity-based direct action strategies that work for our political, social, and legal contexts?" This is a different question than "How do we form hotlines and accompaniment collectives?" although it probably will include asking, "What could accompaniment look like in the United States?" The path from legal to illegal presents different challenges and opportunities than the path to creating safe access in a context of long-term, ongoing restriction. There will not be a single answer to the question of what solidarity looks like and how it shapes action, but we need to keep asking the questions in order to develop strategies that work here, in all the different contexts that make up "here."

Learning from activists across the Global South and parts of Europe does not mean replicating their work, although it might mean understanding why a particular form of action works for particular conditions as a way to ask new questions about our own contexts. We can probably assume there will be a variety of legal threats and perhaps charges against activists as well as people who abort; that is a reason to include a trusted lawyer in your planning, but NOT a reason to avoid doing anything. At least two hotlines in South America had charges filed against them at some point, but nothing came of them for the organizations or individuals. The legal landscape of abortion in the United States changes almost daily right now, which puts extraordinary pressure on lawyers, activists, and people who need abortions—but hunkering down until we see how it all shakes out would guarantee a worse outcome than if we mobilize resistance in an ongoing, flexible, creative, and intersectional way. Local activists in the most affected communities will be central to thinking about what forms of action and solidarity will be useful while not generating additional risk—and activists in states with protective laws will need to be in active dialogue with those in riskier locations in order to build effective, useful networks of solidarity and action.

Direct action based in solidarity and care, in all its various forms, is intrinsically prefigurative, modeling the world that activists envision building in the future. The feminist health movement of the 1960s and '70s was prefigurative in its reimagining of women's health care. The movement for SMA brings demedicalization together with practices of support and care to imagine and create abortion as a process entirely under the control of a person with an undesired pregnancy—an idea that should not be an act of radical imagination, but still is for most of the world. These forms of direct action continue to be radical and prefigurative even under conditions of legality, as a legal abortion can still be performed under conditions of marginalization and lack of respect for the bodily autonomy of the pregnant person. The communal nature of autonomy becomes visible when institutional violence is answered by solidarity to create systems of recognition, support, and accompaniment—and profoundly disrupt the institutional processes that criminalize and dehumanize.

The world envisioned, or prefigured, by this movement is built through deeply feminist understandings of reproductive justice and bodily autonomy: The justice and autonomy envisioned by Black feminists for decades, in which everyone has what they need to build the lives and families they desire in healthy and safe environments; the justice and autonomy envisioned by trans activists as they work to create worlds in which their lives are seen, valued, and respected in all their diversity. The movement for SMA is part of these shared visions of a world that would emerge from an anti-racist feminist and queer politics, with an emphasis on the solidarity, care, and support that enable autonomy as we create paths toward the world we imagine, prefigure, and slowly build. It's hard to imagine a world based on justice when what you see around you looks closer to fascism, but that is precisely when demands for justice have to be made and, indeed, offer the only real pathway out. This is something generations before us have known—and as many feminists in the Global South and feminists of color in the United States know today.

The practice of *acompañamiento* carries layers of meaning in Spanish, and we will need to learn how to translate those meanings and practices into English in the places where we live. We will need to commit to accompanying each other across movements, across regions, across social and economic difference, to find paths forward. Movements sometimes struggle with the gap between what we know is needed versus what we think we can win, but activists have long known that if you start by asking for what you think is "winnable" then you will always lose. Feminists in Ireland, Argentina, Mexico, and Colombia demanded justice and human rights—and won significant victories based on rights, not just protected spaces of "privacy." This is a perilous and unstable time at so many levels, and this calls for—demands—that we get off the path of survival through incremental gains and anchor resistance on the terra firma of justice. We could get more than we ever thought possible.

Acknowledgments

Any book has a social context and a kind of extended family that reflects the intrinsically collective nature of knowledge, of work in all its forms, and perhaps especially of research and writing (which are so often depicted as solitary pursuits when nothing could be farther from the truth). This particular book brings together different periods of my own life, which may give it a larger extended family than some others.

First and foremost, this book would not exist without the active participation of feminist activists in multiple countries and regions who participated in, supported, and enabled this project in countless ways. I can't thank the interview participants by name—anonymity means that I never made a list of who I interviewed and know most of them by first name only—but I am deeply grateful for their interest, their trust, the work that they do, and all that I learned from them. There are, of course, others who I can name who supported this project in many ways. I could write a list but that becomes tedious to read, so I will just call out a few of the many people who made this possible. Huge thanks to: Sara Larrea for introducing me to activists across Latin America; Susan Yanow for encouragement, support, and helping me make connections from the early stages of the project, as well as for ongoing conversation; and Kinga Jelinska for welcoming me to Amsterdam and supporting this project in countless ways (including with Open Society Foundations). To OSF for making it possible to travel as much as I did, and for giving space to my early analysis of the similarities between drug-related harm reduction and self-managed abortion. To Marrisa Velarde for all her work, paid and unpaid, on this project as a research assistant and colleague. To Caitlin Gerdts for ongoing conversations about research and politics. And to Deborrah Dancy, the extraordinary administrative coordinator of the Brooklyn College Sociology Department, who graciously enabled my ridiculous travel schedule when I was both doing fieldwork and serving as chair of the department.

I came to self-managed abortion through many years of work in harm reduction around drugs and HIV, and it feels important to recognize some of the people who were key to that part of my life. Thank you to Lynn Paltrow and NAPW (now Pregnancy Justice) for all the work you have done at the intersections of harm reduction and reproductive justice, and to Lynn for being the person who put needle exchange and reproductive justice activists in a room together to talk about medication abortion back in 2015. Thanks to Caroline Acker for being an amazing travel companion on a slightly crazy exploratory trip in 2016 to see if this project might be possible. To the memory of Carmen Landau (*presente*)—for being herself, for doing a joint presentation with me at NAF in 2017, and for embodying the connections between harm reduction and abortion like it was obvious and no big deal. To reach a little farther back in time, all my love to Moving Equipment: Queer Harm Reduction Collective with whom I learned so much as we formed a contentious and semi-functional activist family while handing out harm-reduction supplies in streets, parks, and abandoned spaces of New York City; in some fundamental ways, this book emerges from the work we did together.

This project has consumed my life in various ways over several years, which would not have been possible without the support and encouragement of my partner, Margaret Reiff, who always said, "Just go, it will be fine," even when I knew that wasn't really what she wanted. And in memory of my maternal grandmother, an immigrant woman who, like countless other women across time, had an abortion when it was not legal but needed to happen anyway—and to whoever helped her get a safe abortion that enabled her to have a long, healthy life afterwards.

Notes

Introduction

1. R. M. Barbosa and M. Arilha, "The Brazilian Experience with Cytotec," *Studies in Family Planning*, vol. 24(4) 1993; R. Gomperts et al., "Provision of Medical Abortion Using Telemedicine in Brazil," *Contraception*, vol. 89(2) 2014; J. Sherris, A. Bingham, M. A. Burns, S. Girvin, E. Westley, and P. I. Gomez, "Misoprostol Use in Developing Countries: Results from a Multicountry Study," *International Journal of Gynecology and Obstetrics*, 88, 2005; M. Wainwright, C. J. Colvin, A. Swartz, and N. Leon, "Self-Management of Medical Abortion: A Qualitative Evidence Synthesis," *Reproductive Health Matters*, vol. 24(47) 2016.
2. N. Braine and M. Velarde, "Self-Managed Abortion: Strategies for Support by a Global Feminist Movement," *Women's Reproductive Health*, vol. 9(3) 2022.
3. M. Castells, *Networks of Outrage and Hope: Social Movements in the Internet Age* (New York: Wiley, 2015).
4. L. Bell and P. O'Hare, "Latin American Politics Underground: Networks, Rhizomes and Resistance in Cartonera Publishing," *International Journal of Cultural Studies*, vol. 23(1) 2020.
5. Center for Reproductive Rights map of abortion law globally: https://maps.reproductiverights.org/worldabortionlaws; A. Bankole, L. Remez, O. Owolabi, J. Philbin, and P. Williams, *From Unsafe to Safe Abortion in Sub-Saharan Africa: Slow but Steady Progress*, report published by the Guttmacher Institute, December 2020.
6. M. Prandini Assis, "Liberating Abortion Pills in Legally Restricted Settings: Activism As Public Criminology," in K. Henne and R. Shah (eds)

Routledge Handbook of Public Criminologies (Oxfordshire: Taylor and Francis, 2020).

7. N. Braine, "Autonomous Health Movements: Criminalization, De-Medicalization, and Community-Based Direct Action," *Health and Human Rights Journal*, vol. 22(2) 2020.
8. B. Winikoff and W. Sheldon, "Use of Medicines Changing the Face of Abortion," *International Perspectives on Sexual and Reproductive Health*, vol. 38(3) 2012; B. Ganatra et al., "Global, Regional, and Subregional Classification of Abortions by Safety, 2010–2014: Estimates from a Bayesian Hierarchical Model," *Lancet*, vol. 390, 2017.
9. D. C. Des Jarlais et al., "Declining Seroprevalence in a Very Large HIV Epidemic: Injecting Drug Users in NYC 1991 to 1996," *American Journal of Public Health*, 88, 1801–6, 1998.

1. Abortion Is Unstoppable

1. R. Petchesky, *Abortion and Woman's Choice: The State, Sexuality, and Reproductive Freedom* (Evanston, IL: Northeastern University Press, 1990).
2. J. Flavin, *Our Bodies, Our Crimes: The Policing of Women's Reproduction in America* (New York: NYU Press, 2009).
3. Petchesky, *Abortion and Woman's Choice*.
4. Flavin, *Our Bodies, Our Crimes*.
5. Flavin, *Our Bodies, Our Crimes*.
6. Petchesky, *Abortion and Woman's Choice*.
7. Petchesky, *Abortion and Woman's Choice*; M. Murphy, *Seizing the Means of Reproduction: Entanglements of Feminism, Health, and Technoscience* (Durham, NC: Duke University Press, 2012).
8. Petchesky, *Abortion and Woman's Choice*.
9. N. Lee, *The Search for an Abortionist* (Chicago: University of Chicago Press, 1969).
10. L. J. Reagan, "Crossing the Border for Abortions: California Activists, Mexican Clinics, and the Creation of a Feminist Health Agency in the 1960s," *Feminist Studies*, vol. 26(2) 2000.
11. H. Stephenson, K. Zeldes, and A. Sweeney, "Write a Chapter and Change the World": How the Boston Women's Health Book Collective Transformed Women's Health Then—and Now," *American Journal of Public Health*, vol. 98(10) 2008.
12. Murphy, *Seizing the Means of Reproduction*.

13. Murphy, *Seizing the Means of Reproduction*; J. Schoen, "Living through Some Great Change: The Establishment of Abortion Services," *American Journal of Public Health*, vol. 103(3) 2013.
14. Schoen, "Living through Some Great Change."
15. S. Yanow, "It Is Time to Integrate Abortion into Primary Care," *American Journal of Public Health*, vol. 103(1) 2013.
16. R. Balmer, "The Real Origins of the Religious Right: They'll Tell You It Was Abortion. Sorry, the Historical Record's Clear: It Was Segregation," *Politico*, May 27, 2014. Randall Balmer is a respected historian of religion, and his academic work can be found in historical journals and books. The *Politico* article cited here summarizes his relevant arguments in a form that is accessible to anyone who is interested. For those who want to learn more, his professional work is available through academic journals and presses.
17. Balmer, "The Real Origins of the Religious Right."
18. NARAL Pro-Choice America website, https://www.prochoiceamerica.org/issue/antiabortion-violence/.
19. L. Kaplan, *The Story of Jane: The Legendary Underground Feminist Abortion Service* (Chicago: University of Chicago Press, 1997).
20. Kaplan, *The Story of Jane*.
21. Murphy, *Seizing the Means of Reproduction*; Women's Health Specialists website, https://www.womenshealthspecialists.org/self-help/menstrual-extraction/.
22. R. Allen and B. M. O'Brien, "Uses of Misoprostol in Obstetrics and Gynecology," *Reviews in Obstetrics and Gynecology*, vol. 2(3) 2009; World Health Organization, *Medical Management of Abortion*, 2018.
23. R. M. Barbosa and M. Arilha, "The Brazilian Experience with Cytotec," *Studies in Family Planning*, vol. 24(4) 1993; S. Zordo, "The Biomedicalization of Illegal Abortion: The Double Life of Misoprostol in Brazil," *Historia, Ciencias, Saude*—Manguinhos Rio de Janeiro, vol. 23(1) 2016.
24. C. Murtagh, E. Wells, E. G. Raymond, F. Coeytaux, and B. Winikoff, "Exploring the Feasibility of Obtaining Mifepristone and Misoprostol from the Internet," *Contraception*, vol. 97(4) 2018.
25. B. Ganatra, et al., "Global, Regional, and Subregional Classification of Abortions by Safety, 2010–2014: Estimates from a Bayesian Hierarchical Model," *Lancet*, vol. 390, 2017.
26. For example: C. Gerdts and I. Hudaya, "Quality of Care in a Safe-Abortion Hotline in Indonesia: Beyond Harm Reduction," *American Journal of Public Health*, vol. 106(11) 2016; S. Larrea, L. Palència, and G. Perez, "Aborto farmacológico dispensado a través de un servicio de telemedicina

a mujeres de América Latina: Complicaciones y su tratamiento," *Gaceta Sanitaria*, 2015; H. Moseson, et al., "Effectiveness of Self-Managed Medication Abortion with Accompaniment Support in Argentina and Nigeria (SAFE): A Prospective, Observational Cohort Study and Non-Inferiority Analysis with Historical Controls," *Lancet Global Health*, vol. 10, 2022.

27. Schoen, "Living through Some Great Change."
28. C. Bercu, et al., "In-Person Later Abortion Accompaniment: A Feminist Collective-Facilitated Self-Care Practice in Latin America," *Sexual and Reproductive Health Matters*, vol. 29(3) 2021; S. Larrea, L. Palencia, and C. Borrell, "Medical Abortion Provision and Quality of Care: What Can Be Learned from Feminist Activists?" *Health Care for Women International*, 2021.
29. L. M. Morgan, "Reproductive Rights or Reproductive Justice? Lessons from Argentina," *Health and Human Rights Journal*, vol. 17(1) 2015.

2. We Are Everywhere

1. R. Petchesky, *Abortion and Woman's Choice: The State, Sexuality, and Reproductive Freedom* (Boston: Northeastern University Press, 1990).
2. M. Gilmartin and S. Kennedy, "A Double Movement: The Politics of Reproductive Mobility in Ireland," in C. Sethna and G. Davis (eds) *Abortion across Borders: Transnational Travel and Access to Abortion Services* (Baltimore: Johns Hopkins University Press, 2019); A. Ignaciuk, "Abortion Travel and the Cost of Reproductive Choice in Spain," in Sethna and Davis (eds) *Abortion across Borders*.
3. E. Ciaputa, "Abortion and the Catholic Church in Poland," in Sethna and Davis (eds) *Abortion across Borders*.
4. Ciaputa, "Abortion and the Catholic Church in Poland."
5. Gilmartin and Kennedy, "A Double Movement"; A. R. A. Aiken, I. Digol, J. Trussell, and R. Gomperts, "Self Reported Outcomes and Adverse Events after Medical Abortion through Online Telemedicine: Population Based Study in the Republic of Ireland and Northern Ireland," *BMJ* (Online), 357, 2017.
6. E. Brookman-Amissah and J. Banda Moyo, "Abortion Law Reform in Sub-Saharan Africa: No Turning Back," *Reproductive Health Matters*, vol. 12(24 supplement) 2004.
7. M. Prandini Assis, "Liberating Abortion Pills in Legally Restricted Settings: Activism As Public Criminology," in K. Henne and R. Shah (eds) *Routledge Handbook of Public Criminologies*, 2020.

8. H. Moseson, S. Herold, S. Filippa, J. Barr-Walker, S. E. Baum, and C. Gerdts, "Self-Managed Abortion: A Systemic Scoping Review," *Best Practice and Research Clinical Obstetrics and Gynecology*, vol. 63, 2020.
9. Brookman-Amissah and Moyo, "Abortion Law Reform in Sub-Saharan Africa."
10. A. Bankole, L. Remez, O. Owolabi, J. Philbin, and P. Williams, *From Unsafe to Safe Abortion in Sub-Saharan Africa: Slow but Steady Progress*, report published by the Guttmacher Institute, December 2020.
11. Bankole, Remez, Owolabi, Philbin, and Williams, *From Unsafe to Safe Abortion in Sub-Saharan Africa*.
12. K. J. Kaoma, *Colonizing African Values: How the Christian Right Is Transforming Sexual Politics in Africa*, Political Research Associates 2012; L. Morgan, *The Sovereignty Strategy: Antiabortion Politics in the Americas*, Political Research Associates, 2022.
13. All statistics from the World Health Organization map of HIV prevalence estimates worldwide in November 2022.
14. E. Bass, *To End a Plague: America's Fight to Defeat AIDS in Africa* (New York: Public Affairs Press, 2021).
15. L. Namibiru and K. S. Wepukhulu, *US Christian Right Pours More Than $50m into Africa: Conservative Groups Increase Their Spending and Activity in What Critics Call an "Opportunistic Use of Africans" for US-Style "Culture Wars,"* openDemocracy, October 29, 2020; Jasper Jackson, *Unholy Alliance: The Far-Right Religious Network Attacking Reproductive and LGBTQ+ Rights*, The Bureau of Investigative Journalism, September 25, 2022.
16. Namibiru and Wepukhulu, *US Christian Right Pours More Than $50m into Africa*; D. Cariboni and T. Hovhannisyan, *In a Case at the Inter-American Court of Human Rights, European Groups Supported Criminalizing Women Who Had Obstetric Emergencies*, openDemocracy, December 3, 2021.
17. *Explorando el activism vinculado al aborto seguro a traves de las experiencias e historias de feministas que integran las redes de acompanamiento en America Latina*, Disponible en el sitio de web de *Las Socorristas*.

3. An Act of Solidarity between Women

1. M. Prandini Assis, "Liberating Abortion Pills in Legally Restricted Settings: Activism As Public Criminology," in K. Henne and R. Shah (eds) *Routledge Handbook of Public Criminologies* (Oxfordshire: Taylor and Francis, 2020).
2. L. Kaplan, *The Story of Jane: The Legendary Underground Feminist Abortion Service* (Chicago: University of Chicago Press, 1997).

3. Kaplan, *The Story of Jane.*
4. *Bans on Specific Abortion Methods Used after the First Trimester*, report by Guttmacher Institute, November 1, 2022; R. Zurbriggen, N. Vacarezza, G. Alonso, B. Grosso, and M. Trpin, *El aborto con medicamentos en el segundo trimester de embarazo: una investigacion socorrista feminista*, La Parte Maldita, Buenos Aires, 2018.
5. Zurbriggen, Vacarezza, Alonso, Grosso, and Trpin, *El aborto con medicamentos en el segundo trimester*; C. Gerdts, R. T. Jayaweera, S. E. Baum and I. Hudaya, "Second-Trimester Medication Abortion outside the Clinic Setting: An Analysis of Electronic Client Records from a Safe Abortion Hotline in Indonesia," *BMJ Sexual and Reproductive Health*, vol. 44(4), 2018.
6. Zurbriggen, Vacarezza, Alonso, Grosso, and Trpin, *El aborto con medicamentos en el segundo*; H. Moseson et al., "Effectiveness of Self-Managed Medication Abortion with Accompaniment Support in Argentina and Nigeria (SAFE): A Prospective, Observational Cohort Study and Non-Inferiority Analysis with Historical Controls," *Lancet Global Health*, vol. 10, 2022; C. Gerdts, *Expanding Abortion Access: Understanding the Evidence on and People's Experiences with Self-Managed Abortion*, presentation at European Access Project Conference, Barcelona, Spain, June 22–23, 2022.
7. J. Espinoza Escarate, *Viviana Diaz de Con las amigas y en la casa: "Creo que toda feminista deberia acompañar un aborto*," Entrevista publicado en el sitio de Observatorio y Genero, September 24, 2019.
8. C. Bercu et al., "In-Person Later Abortion Accompaniment: A Feminist Collective-Facilitated Self-Care Practice in Latin America," *Sexual and Reproductive Health Matters*, vol. 29(3) 2021.
9. L. Presser, "A Secret Network of Women Is Working Outside the Law and the Medical Establishment to Provide Safe, Cheap Home Abortions," *California Sunday Magazine*, March 28, 2018.
10. F. Coeytaux, L. Hessini, N. Ejano, A. Obbuyi, M. Oguttu, J. Osur, and K. Shuken, "Facilitating Women's Access to Misoprostol through Community-Based Advocacy in Kenya and Tanzania," *International Journal of Gynecology and Obstetrics*, vol. 125(1) 2014.

4. Being an Activist Is Not Easy

1. M. Prandini Assis, "Liberating Abortion Pills in Legally Restricted Settings: Activism As Public Criminology," in K. Henne and R. Shah (eds) *Routledge Handbook of Public Criminologies* (Oxfordshire: Taylor and Francis, 2020).

2. F. Coeytaux, L. Hessini, N. Ejano, A. Obbuyi, M. Oguttu, J. Osur, and K. Shuken, "Facilitating Women's Access to Misoprostol through Community-Based Advocacy in Kenya and Tanzania," *International Journal of Gynecology and Obstetrics*, vol. 125(1) 2014.
3. M. Alexander, *The New Jim Crow: Mass Incarceration in the Age of Colorblindness* (New York: The New Press, 2010).
4. L. Huss, F. Diaz-Tello, and G. Samari, *Self-Care, Criminalized: August 2022 Preliminary Findings*, report released by If/When/How: Lawyering for Reproductive Justice, 2022.
5. D. Cariboni and T. Hovhannisyan, *In a Case at the Inter-American Court of Human Rights, European Groups Supported Criminalizing Women Who Had Obstetric Emergencies*, openDemocracy, December 3, 2021.
6. E. Ciaputa, "Abortion and the Catholic Church in Poland," in C. Sethna and G. Davis (eds) *Abortion across Borders: Transnational Travel and Access to Abortion Services* (Baltimore: Johns Hopkins University Press, 2019).
7. *Profile on the Right: CitizenGo*, Political Research Associates, May 4, 2018.
8. L. Namibiru and K. S. Wepukhulu, *US Christian Right Pours More Than $50m into Africa: Conservative Groups Increase Their Spending and Activity in What Critics Call an "Opportunistic Use of Africans" for US-Style "Culture Wars,"* openDemocracy, October 29, 2020; *Profiles on the Right: World Congress of Families*, Political Research Associates, November 4, 2013.
9. Namibiru and Wepukhulu, *US Christian Right Pours More Than $50m into Africa*.
10. C. Bercu et al., "In-Person Later Abortion Accompaniment: A Feminist Collective-Facilitated Self-Care Practice in Latin America," *Sexual and Reproductive Health Matters*, vol. 29(3) 2021.

5. We Have Become the Experts

1. B. Dangl, *The Price of Fire: Resource Wars and Social Movements in Bolivia* (Chico, CA: AK Press, 2007); T. Lewis, *Ecuador's Environmental Revolutions: Ecoimperialists, Ecodependents, and Ecoresisters* (Cambridge: MIT Press, 2016).
2. M. Murphy, *Seizing the Means of Reproduction: Entanglements of Feminism, Health, and Technoscience* (Durham, NC: Duke University Press, 2012).
3. B. Ehrenreich and D. English, *Witches, Midwives and Nurses* (New York: Feminist Press, 2010).
4. R. Zurbriggen, N. Vacarezza, G. Alonso, B. Grosso, and M. Trpin, *El aborto con medicamentos en el segundo trimester de embarazo: una investigacion socorrista feminista*, La Parte Maldita, Buenos Aires, 2018.

5. H. Moseson et al., "Effectiveness of Self-Managed Medication Abortion with Accompaniment Support in Argentina and Nigeria (SAFE): A Prospective, Observational Cohort Study and Non-Inferiority Analysis with Historical Controls," *Lancet Global Health* vol. 10, 2022; C. Bercu et al., "In-Person Later Abortion Accompaniment: A Feminist Collective-Facilitated Self-Care Practice in Latin America," *Sexual and Reproductive Health Matters*, vol. 29(3) 2021.
6. Zurbriggen, Vacarezza, Alonso, Grosso, and Trpin, *El aborto con medicamentos en el segundo trimester de embarazo*; C. Gerdts, *Expanding Abortion Access: Understanding the Evidence on and People's Experiences with Self-Managed Abortion*, presentation at European Access Project Conference, Barcelona, Spain, June 22–23, 2022.
7. Zurbriggen, Vacarezza, Alonso, Grosso, and Trpin, *El aborto con medicamentos en el segundo trimester de embarazo*.
8. Murphy, *Seizing the Means of Reproduction*; J. Schoen, "Living through Some Great Change: The Establishment of Abortion Services," *American Journal of Public Health*, vol. 103(3) 2013.
9. N. Braine, *Factors Shaping Implementation of Overdose Prevention in Drug Treatment*, report prepared for the New York State Department of Health, AIDS Institute, 2008.
10. D. Grossman et al., *Texas Policy Evaluation Project Research Brief: Knowledge, Opinion, and Experience Related to Self-Induction in Texas*, presented at the North American Forum on Family Planning, Chicago, November 14, 2015.
11. L. Ralph et al., "Prevalence of Self-Managed Abortion among Women of Reproductive Age in the United States," *Journal of the American Medical Association*, Network Open, vol. 3(12) December 1, 2020.
12. R. K. Jones and J. Jerman, "Population Group Abortion Rates and Lifetime Incidence of Abortion: United States, 2008–2014," *American Journal of Public Health*, 2017.
13. I. Palma, C. Moreno, A. Álvarez, and A. Richards, "Experience of Clandestine Use of Medical Abortion among University Students in Chile: A Qualitative Study," *Contraception*, vol. 97(100) 2018.
14. N. Braine, "Autonomous Health Movements: Criminalization, De-Medicalization, and Community-Based Direct Action," *Health and Human Rights Journal*, vol. 22(2) 2022.
15. A. R. A. Aiken, I. Digol, J. Trussell, and R. Gomperts, "Self Reported Outcomes and Adverse Events after Medical Abortion through Online Telemedicine: Population Based Study in the Republic of Ireland and Northern Ireland," *BMJ* (online), 357, 2017; A. Aiken, K. A. Guthrie, M.

Schellekens, J. Trussell, and R. Gomperts, "Barriers to Accessing Abortion Services and Perspectives on Using Mifepristone and Misoprostol at Home in Great Britain," *Contraception*, vol. 97(2) 2018; S. Larrea, L. Palència, and G. Perez, "Aborto farmacológico dispensado a través de un servicio de telemedicina a mujeres de América Latina: Complicaciones y su tratamiento," *Gaceta Sanitari*, 2015; A. Wollum, S. Larrea, C. Gerdts, and K. Jelinska, "Requests for Medication Abortion Support during and after the Zika Epidemic," *Global Public Health*, vol. 16(3) 2021.

16. C. Gerdts and I. Hudaya, "Quality of Care in a Safe-Abortion Hotline in Indonesia: Beyond Harm Reduction," *American Journal of Public Health*, vol. 106(11) 2016.
17. S. Larrea, L. Palencia, and C. Borrell, "Medical Abortion Provision and Quality of Care: What Can Be Learned from Feminist Activists?" *Health Care for Women International*, 2021.
18. C. Bercu et al., "In-Person Later Abortion Accompaniment."
19. H. Moseson et al., "Studying Accompaniment Model Feasibility and Effectiveness (SAFE) Study: Study Protocol for a Prospective Observational Cohort Study of the Effectiveness of Self-Managed Medication Abortion," *BMJ Open*, vol. 11(10) 2020; H. Moseson et al., "Effectiveness of Self-Managed Medication Abortion with Accompaniment Support in Argentina and Nigeria."

7. In It for the Long Term

1. L. Bunnage, "Social Movement Engagement over the Long Haul: Understanding Activist Retention," *Sociology Compass*, vol. 8(4) 2014.

Index